Teach.
Inspire...
Lead...

MW00388159

With REA's PRAXIS II® Elementary Education test prep, you'll be in a class all your own.

We'd like to hear from you!
Send your comments to *info@rea.com*.

Research & Education Association

The Best Teachers' Test Preparation for the

PRAXIS II®

Elementary Education:
Content Area Exercises (0012)

Julie O'Connell, M.A.
Department of English
Seton Hall University
South Orange, NJ

Visit our Educator Support Center at:
www.REA.com/teacher

For updates to the test and this book visit: www.rea.com/praxis/eled12.htm

Planet Friendly Publishing
✔ Made in the United States
✔ Printed on Recycled Paper
Text: 10%   Cover: 10%
Learn more: www.greenedition.org

At REA we're committed to producing books in an earth-friendly manner and to helping our customers make greener choices.

Manufacturing books in the United States ensures compliance with strict environmental laws and eliminates the need for international freight shipping, a major contributor to global air pollution.

And printing on recycled paper helps minimize our consumption of trees, water and fossil fuels. This book was printed on paper made with **10% post-consumer waste**. According to Environmental Defense's Paper Calculator, by using this innovative paper instead of conventional papers, we achieved the following environmental benefits:

Trees Saved: 4 • Air Emissions Eliminated: 845 pounds
Water Saved: 873 gallons • Solid Waste Eliminated: 250 pounds

For more information on our environmental practices, please visit us online at **www.rea.com/green**

Research & Education Association
61 Ethel Road West
Piscataway, New Jersey 08854
E-mail: info@rea.com

**The Best Teachers' Test Preparation for the
PRAXIS II® Elementary Education:
Content Area Exercises (0012)**

Printed in the United States of America

Library of Congress Control Number 2009927259

ISBN-13: 978-0-7386-0399-5
ISBN-10: 0-7386-0399-6

The competencies presented in this book were created and implemented by Educational Testing Service. For individual state requirements, consult your state education agency. For further information visit the PRAXIS website at www.ets.org. PRAXIS II® and The PRAXIS Series™ are trademarks of ETS®.

REA® is a registered trademark of
Research & Education Association, Inc.

About Research & Education Association

Founded in 1959, Research & Education Association is dedicated to publishing the finest and most effective educational materials—including software, study guides, and test preps—for students in middle school, high school, college, graduate school, and beyond.

REA's Test Preparation series includes books and software for all academic levels in almost all disciplines. Research & Education Association publishes test preps for students who have not yet entered high school, as well as for high school students preparing to enter college. Students from countries around the world seeking to attend college in the United States will find the assistance they need in REA's publications. For college students seeking advanced degrees, REA publishes test preps for many major graduate school admission examinations in a wide variety of disciplines, including engineering, law, and medicine. Students at every level, in every field, with every ambition can find what they are looking for among REA's publications.

REA's practice tests are always based upon the most recently administered exams and include every type of question that you can expect on the actual exams.

REA's publications and educational materials are highly regarded and continually receive an unprecedented amount of praise from professionals, instructors, librarians, parents, and students. Our authors are as diverse as the fields represented in the books we publish. They are well-known in their respective disciplines and serve on the faculties of prestigious high schools, colleges, and universities throughout the United States and Canada.

Today, REA's wide-ranging catalog is a leading resource for teachers, students, and professionals.

We invite you to visit us at *www.rea.com* to find out how "REA is making the world smarter."

Acknowledgments

We would like to thank Larry Kling, Vice President, Editorial, for his editorial direction; Pam Weston, Vice President, Publishing, for setting the quality standards for production integrity and managing the publication to completion; Kathleen Casey, Senior Editor, for project management; Christine Saul, Senior Graphic Artist, for cover design; and Rachel DiMatteo, Graphic Artist, post-production file mapping.

We also gratefully acknowledge Alison Minion for copyediting, DataStream Content Solutions for typesetting, the Editors of REA for proofreading, and Terry Casey for indexing the manuscript.

About the Author

Julie O'Connell, M.A., teaches English at Seton Hall University. A doctoral candidate at Drew University, she is currently writing her dissertation entitled "Narrative Self-Representations by Writers with Asperger's Syndrome." Ms. O'Connell holds a master's degree from Brown University and a bachelor's degree in English from Georgetown University. For ten years, she served as the Director of the Felician College Writing Lab where she initiated and oversaw an interdisciplinary college writing center which used a Writing Across the Curriculum philosophy. Ms. O'Connell also developed and taught a ten week Praxis II Elementary Education preparation course for Teacher Education students.

Ms. O'Connell, listed in *Who's Who Among America's Teachers*, has taught college courses in developmental writing, rhetoric and composition, literature, reading, ESL, and Business Communications. She has worked as a Learning Specialist at a large public university, and taught high school English. She's given numerous presentations on learning styles, study strategies, time management, test preparation, test taking, note taking, and reading skills for undergraduate students. She has a special interest in working with students who have learning disabilities and who face other kinds of academic challenges. She has been honored in Who's Who Among America's Teachers.

Author's Acknowledgements

This book would not have been possible without the help of certain individuals who consistently went out of their way to help me write it.

I dedicate it to my beautiful daughters, Jennifer and Catherine Juliano, who sacrificed many nights away from me when I was at the library or dining room table. Thank you for understanding.

First, I would like to thank Scott Juliano for his ongoing support and for his help with the mathematics and science sections of the book. I thank Jennifer Jarvis Phillips, Director of Curriculum at Far Hills Country Day School, for her content editing of the Language Arts and Practice Test sections. Thanks to Glen Coleman for his unparalleled content editing of the Social Studies section. I would also like to thank the Sisters of Felician College—as a result of my employment for you, I had the great opportunity to assist students who were preparing for the Praxis exam. These students inspired me through their perseverance, and we learned so much together. I want to thank the Teacher Education department of Felician College for encouraging me to develop the course. I would also like to salute the inspirational teachers who helped me formulate the initial curriculum: Ann Babliot, the most generous person I know, Kefang Yang for her giftedness in mathematics and economics, and Naa Kai Tagoe, a born science teacher. I also thank all of the students of those early Praxis reviews, specifically Lucia Mahupe, Sister Davina, and Wanda Kopic: your hard work continues to inspire me to keep trying. Lastly, I thank my father, John F. O'Connell, for reviewing my work throughout this process and for giving me incalculable suggestions. Dad, everything I know about writing, I learned from you—you will always be my first and last writing teacher.

I am filled with gratitude for the expertise and friendship that all of you have given me.

CONTENTS

Introduction

The Praxis II Elementary Education: Content Area Exercises 0012 is the third in REA's series of Praxis II Elementary Education test preps, and is complementary to REA's PRAXIS II Elementary Education (0011) and (0014) titles. Think of this book as your toolkit to pass the test. It will help take the mystery and anxiety out of the testing process by equipping you not only with the nuts and bolts, but also, ultimately, with the confidence to succeed alongside your peers across the United States. We at REA have put a lot of thought into this, and the result is a book that pulls together all the critical information you need to know to pass the Praxis II Elementary Education: Content Area Exercises 0012 test. Let us help you fill in the blanks—literally and figuratively! We will provide you with the touchstones that will allow you to do your very best come test day and beyond. In this guide, REA offers our customarily in-depth, up-to-date, objective coverage, with test-specific modules devoted to targeted review and realistic practice exams complete with the kind of detail that makes a difference when you're coming down the homestretch in your preparation.

ABOUT THE PRAXIS SERIES

Praxis is the Educational Testing Service's (ETS) shorthand for Professional Assessments for Beginning Teachers. The Praxis Series is a group of teacher-licensing tests that ETS developed in concert with states across the nation. There are three categories of tests in the series: Praxis I, Praxis II and Praxis III. Praxis I includes the paper-based Pre-Professional Skills Tests (PPST) and the Praxis I Computer-Based Tests (CBT). Both versions cover essentially the same subject matter. These exams measure reading, mathematics, and writing skills and are often a requirement for admission to a teacher education program. Praxis II embraces Subject Assessment/Specialty Area Tests, including the Praxis II Social Studies series, of which the Praxis II Elementary Education: Content Area Exercises 0012 exam is a part. The Praxis II examinations cover the subject matter that students typically study in teacher education courses such as, human growth and development, school curriculum, methods of teaching, and other professional development courses. In most teacher-training programs, students take these tests after having completed their classroom training, the course work, and practicum. Praxis III is different from the multiple-choice and essay tests typically used for assessment purposes. With this assessment, ETS-trained observers evaluate an instructor's performance in the classroom, using nationally validated criteria. The observers may videotape the lesson, and other teaching experts may critique the resulting tapes.

HOW TO USE THIS BOOK

What Do I Study First?

Read over REA's subject reviews and suggestions for test taking. Studying the reviews thoroughly will reinforce the basic skills you will need to do well on the exams. Make sure to do the practice exams in this book so that you will be familiar with the format and procedures involved with taking the actual test.

When Should I Start Studying?

It is never too early to start studying. The earlier you begin, the more time you will have to sharpen your skills. Do not procrastinate! Cramming is not an effective way to study because it does not allow you the time needed to learn the test material.

ABOUT THE TEST

The Praxis II Elementary Education: Content Area Exercises (0012) test is required in seven U.S. states: Connecticut, Hawaii, Maryland, Nevada, North Carolina, Rhode Island,

and South Carolina. Unlike the 0014 exam, which assesses K-6 curricular content in a multiple-choice exam, and the 0011 test, which evaluates curriculum, instruction, and assessment in a multiple-choice test, the 0012 exam requires longer and more insightful responses to problems (i.e., content area exercises) that are presented.

Who Takes the Test?

Most people who take the Praxis II Elementary Education: Content Area Exercises (0012) are seeking initial licensure. You should check with your state's education agency to determine which Praxis examination(s) you should take. The ETS Praxis website (*www.ets.org/praxis/*) and registration bulletin may also help you determine the test(s) you need to take for certification. You should also consult your education program for its own test requirements. Remember that colleges and universities often require Praxis examinations for entry into programs, for graduation, and for the completion of a teacher certification program. These requirements may differ from the baseline requirements the state has for teacher certification. You will need to meet both sets of requirements.

When Should I Take the Test?

The Praxis II Elementary Education 0012 is a test for those who have completed or almost completed their teacher education programs. Each state establishes its own requirements for certification: some states specify the passing of other tests; some states may require the test for initial certification; and other states may require the test for beginning teachers during their first months on the job. Generally, each college and university establishes its own requirements for program admission and for graduation. Some colleges and universities require certain tests for graduation and/or for completion of a teacher education program. Check with your college and the state teacher certification agency for details.

When and Where Can I Take the Test?

ETS offers the Praxis II tests seven times a year at a number of locations across the nation. The usual testing day is Saturday, but examinees may request an administration on an alternate day if a conflict—such as a religious obligation—exists.

> **PRAXIS Pointer**
>
> Be prepared, know what the test covers. Don't waste time on "beat-the-test" strategies. Organize a study schedule and keep to it—you will avoid test anxiety.

How Do I Get More Information on the ETS Praxis Exams?

To receive information on upcoming administrations of the Praxis II Elementary Education 0012 test or any other test consult the ETS registration bulletin or website. Contact ETS at:

Educational Testing Service
Teaching and Learning Division
P.O. Box 6051
Princeton, NJ 08541-6051
Phone: (609) 771-7395
Website: *www.ets.org/praxis*
E-mail: *praxis@ets.org*

Special accommodations are available for candidates who are visually impaired, hearing impaired, physically disabled, or specific learning disabled. For questions concerning disability services, contact:

ETS Disability Services: (609) 771-7780
TTY only: (609) 771-7714

Provisions are also available for examinees whose primary language is not English. The ETS registration bulletin and website include directions for those requesting such accommodations. You can also consult ETS with regard to available test sites; reporting test scores; requesting changes in tests, centers, and dates of test; purchasing additional score reports; retaking tests; and other basic facts.

Is There a Registration Fee?

To take a Praxis examination, you must pay a registration fee, which is payable by check, money order, or with American Express, Discover, MasterCard, or Visa credit cards. In certain cases, ETS offers fee waivers. The registration bulletin and website give qualifications for receiving this benefit and describe the application process. Cash is not accepted for payment.

Can I Retake the Test?

Some states, institutions, and associations limit the number of times you can retest. Contact your state or licensing authority to confirm their retest policies.

FORMAT OF THE TEST

Students must write four essays over the course of two hours. Consequently, each of the four 30-minute exercises counts for 25 percent of the test. The questions concern:

Reading and Language Arts
Mathematics
Science or Social Studies
Interdisciplinary Instruction

It is important for anyone preparing for this test to demonstrate not only knowledge of the content of each subject, but also theoretical reasons and methodological practice that can be used in a classroom setting. To that end, this book will provide not only curricular content, but will also summarize current methods for teaching and evaluating that content. Chapter 2 will cover Reading and Language Arts. While much of the chapter will discuss teaching reading, it will also include methods and rationales for teaching writing and spelling. Chapter 3 will review content and teaching strategies for Mathematics. Chapter 4 will cover the areas of Science and Social Studies. Chapter 5 will address the area of Interdisciplinary Instruction. Finally, two full-length practice tests (with responses) are included in Chapter 6.

Before we examine the subject areas, it is important to consider the task at hand when it comes to answering the test questions. The 0012 questions are presented in the form of specific teaching situations in which the writer is asked to discuss an instructional approach, develop an instructional goal, or solve a pedagogical problem by outlining the steps to achieve that goal or solve that problem. In essence, ETS is using a Problem-Based Learning (PBL) approach in this assessment. As Macdonald and Savin-Baden (2004) explain, this type of assessment places the test taker in the future classroom context in order to assess what the professional will do in practice. This kind of task asks the writer not only to remember the important content he or she has learned, but also to synthesize that information with skills and experiences gleaned from classroom observations, student teaching, and prepared lessons. Thus, it is important for the test taker to recall these important teacher education experiences when constructing a response. In short, this test asks you to activate prior knowledge and then to elaborate on what you would do in a particular pedagogical situation. A problem or a series of problems is presented to the test taker. While the situation is challenging, it is also a real-life scenario, and the test taker must reflect on that situation and suggest meaningful ways to address it.

Given the challenges of this type of assessment, how might you write a solid response to this kind of essay question? It helps to first understand the format of these questions. The test question is presented first as a scenario, followed by a series of questions asking the test taker to address that scenario. For example:

In a third grade class, students are preparing to write an Animal Report. Each student has read about his or her animal in books and on the Internet. Each student has been asked to re-read the information and write down important facts about the animal in a chart.

> *List five important steps the students can follow in an effort to help them use the writing process to complete their reports.*

> *Describe two ways the teacher could further assist the students in the classroom. The first example should suggest a way to help the students with written expression. The second example should suggest a way to help them with mechanics.*

How should you approach this question? The following steps will help you break down the scenario.

Read the question.   The most important thing to remember when you are answering an essay question is that you need to read the entire question and answer all parts of the question. In order to read the question very closely, you must recognize key words and phrases in the question. You should be on the lookout for these key words, underline them, and realize what they are asking you to do.

In our example, the writer is being asked to list five steps and describe two ways—one being with written expression and the other with mechanics. Commonly used key words in these types of questions include the following:

DESCRIBE—means examine, analyze, and present your understanding of the situation by including details. Here's a different example that asks the student to describe. The answer models what might be the introductory paragraph to the response.

> Example: *Describe* scaffolding and discuss how it can be used when teaching persuasive writing in a 5th grade classroom.

> Answer: Scaffolding is the idea that teachers provide temporary assistance to students by demonstrating strategies and then eventually shift-

ing the responsibility of the task onto the student. A fifth grade teacher can provide scaffolding to her students by generating a list of structured questions and eventually encouraging students to generate their own questions of inquiry. This essay will explain how that process can take place.

EXPLAIN—means to analyze the problem and interpret an approach by breaking it into parts and giving examples and details to support your answer.

Example: *Explain* three approaches you would take to support emergent reading in a kindergarten classroom.

Answer: Emergent reading is a theory that in the first five years of life, literacy develops gradually as children emerge from being nonreaders to being readers. While there are numerous strategies a kindergarten teacher should employ in a classroom of emergent readers, three important ones are shared reading, partner reading, and using a word wall.

Understand what the question is asking. Look at it to see how it is broken down into parts. Let's go back to our initial test taking example:

In a third grade class, students are preparing to write an Animal Report. Each student has read about his or her animal in books and on the Internet. Each student has been asked to re-read the information and write down important facts about the animal in a chart.

> *List five important steps the students can follow in an effort to help them use the writing process to complete their reports.*

> *Describe two ways the teacher could further assist the students in the classroom. The first example should suggest a way to help the students with written expression. The second example should suggest a way to help them with mechanics.*

What is this question really asking you to do? It seems that the question is asking you to envision a research situation and to evaluate where the students are in the process. Then, you are being asked to see that process through by explaining five more steps that would guide the students through to the finish line: the research report. You are also being asked to explain two classroom approaches you would take to help students with the expression and mechanics of writing.

Plan your time.   Say to yourself "I'm going to brainstorm my ideas and write an outline for the next ten minutes. Then, I'm going to write for fifteen minutes. Finally, I will proof-read for the remaining five minutes."

Brainstorm.   Jot down your ideas for the response. Make sure that you provide reasons for your assertions. Underline key words in your brainstorm.

For our sample question, here is an example of a list of ideas from initial brainstorming.

- Give students an outline to follow of specific things I want them to look for in their own animal—this is a kind of scaffolding—I'd want them to ultimately learn this skill and be able to do it on their own later.
- They should include scientific name of the animal, group it is from, what it looks like, what it eats, where it lives, and its predators.
- Perhaps with the outline they could go back to their sources and look for additional information to take notes on. I could do this as a concept map.
- Drafting should be at least four paragraphs. I could do the four square method for that.
- I'd like them to peer edit. I could make a page they could follow and pair them up according to strengths and weaknesses each student has.
- For the two classroom activities, I could ask students to read their writing aloud to me, we could edit in a conference situation (this will help with mechanics), I could ask students to type their drafts on the computer and use spell check and grammar check. For written expression—I could write comments on drafts and conference with students to tell them where to go further.

Come up with an outline.   Your outline is your best plan of attack. An ideal outline is a well-organized response that collects your thoughts in preparation for writing your actual essay. The outline will flow naturally from the words underlined in your brainstorming notes.

1. Introduction
2. Five Steps:

    a. Give them my outline with specific questions they are all looking to answer.

    b. Concept map

    c. Four Square Method

    d. Drafting

    e. Peer Editing

3. Two classroom approaches:

    a. Conferences about where they can go further and to help them edit—expression

    b. Using the computer in the classroom to type up drafts (spell/grammar check)— mechanics

Structure your response.   You need to have an introduction that briefly and succinctly explains what you will be arguing: this is your central claim. An easy way to do this is to "turn the question around" by making sure that you not only understand what it is asking but also that you have indicated what position you will take regarding it. For example:

> Introduction: There are many approaches a teacher of third grade students can use in showing his or her students how to write a research report about a specific animal. The following five steps and two classroom approaches will demonstrate how the teacher can help students write thorough and balanced reports.

Then, each paragraph you write needs to be guided by a topic sentence that not only references back to your introduction but also is supported by details, examples, and evidence. Ideas need to be connected to other ideas by using transitional words, phrases, and sentences.

Examples of transitional words: first, second, third, finally, in addition, furthermore, moreover, therefore, thus, consequently, in short, in summary, overall

Finally, you need to include a conclusion that restates the main points that you have made and summarizes where you have taken the reader.

Write your response. Make sure that you are thoroughly and concisely answering the question by providing details that indicate that you understand content, theory, and practice. Get to the point and express your ideas simply and clearly. Present evidence to back up your claims. Avoid fancy language and over the top vocabulary. Also, don't fill your answer with unnecessary information, and avoid repeating yourself. Your reader will recognize if you are padding your response. Don't challenge the premise of the question or try to change the question. Stay on topic and demonstrate your knowledge of the field. Write quickly and legibly—you won't have time to re-copy your answer.

> **PRAXIS Pointer**
>
> **Assess how well you know the content of the test. Gather materials that will help you prepare. Don't forget about textbooks and class notes—they are invaluable resources.**

This is the final response to the Animal Report scenario.

While there are many approaches a third grade teacher can use in showing students how to write a detailed research report about a specific animal, the following five steps and two classroom approaches will explain how he or she can help students to write thorough and balanced animal reports.

At this point in the research process, the students have selected an animal, done some reading, and taken notes. Initially, I would give students an outline of specific things I want them to look for as they are researching their own animals. I realize that this is what Lev Vgotsky would refer to as a kind of scaffolding: it's a skill I want to show them now in the hopes that they will be able to do it on their own later. In the outline I'd give them, I would ask students to look for the scientific name of the animal, the group it is from, what it looks like, what it eats, where it lives, and what its predators are. They could use the outline to go back to their sources, look for additional information, and take more notes. Next, I would model for students what the outline would look like as a concept map, and then have them make their own maps of the information. Since I want their drafts to be at least four paragraphs, I would show the students the four square method to give them a graphic organizer prior to drafting. After the drafting process, I'd ask them to peer edit.

I could make a page they could follow and pair them up according to the various strengths and weaknesses of each student.

For my two classroom activities, I would write comments on the drafts and conference with them individually, first listening to them read aloud and then showing them what works and also where they could expand. In my conference, I'd use the PQP method whereby I'd encourage them (praise), point out areas for further clarification (question), and show them areas that need more attention (polish). This approach would help them with their written expression. Secondly, after giving them a mini-lesson on how to cite their sources using a bibliographic entry, I would try to help them with mechanics by asking them to type their drafts and bibliographies on the computer and use spell check and grammar check.

Overall, I believe these approaches would help my third grade students to gain a deeper understanding of the writing process as it relates to research. They will have taken notes on facts, organized those facts into an outline, written a draft, edited it, and composed a final copy, including a bibliography.

Re-read it to revise sentences and to proofread for sentence level errors. There may be sentences that need to be refined for greater clarity. You may have accidentally omitted words. Or, there may be mistakes in spelling, grammar, and mechanics that need to be addressed before the thirty minutes are up. Don't forget to plan your time to allow for this final step.

A recap of the steps we've looked at here:

1. *Read the question.* Underline key words.
2. *Understand what the question is asking.*
3. *Plan your time.*
4. *Brainstorm and underline key ideas.*
5. *Come up with an outline.*
6. *Structure your response.* Introduction, body with transitions, and conclusion.
7. *Write your response.*
8. *Re-read it to revise sentences and to proofread for sentence level errors.*

It's important to note that all of this happens in the ideal scenario, and you may not have enough time for every aspect of the writing process mentioned here. Nevertheless, at the very minimum you should plan your answer (7–10 minutes), answer the question (15 minutes), include an introduction to that answer, write clearly, and proofread (last 5 minutes).

HOW WILL THE RESPONSES BE SCORED?

ETS invites seasoned educators to score the 0012 examinations based on a six-point, holistic grading rubric. These test evaluators are "normed," which means that the group reads, scores, and discusses some papers together. They engage in a conversation about what kind of an essay merits what kind of a score. By discussing responses and practicing the evaluation process together, an effort towards greater consistency and consensus is made. As a result, evaluators understand how an essay earns a score at each stage of the rubric. Another important measure taken by ETS: essays are read by two evaluators with the first scorer's decision hidden from the second scorer; each response is awarded points by adding those two scores together. If the evaluators differ from each other by more than one point, a third, more advanced party is brought in to evaluate the essay, and the score is determined based on that individual's unbiased input.

Scoring Rubric

Score	Comment
6	This response not only answers the question clearly, it also shows superior understanding of the subject matter, human growth and development, and pedagogy. The answer is organized and key ideas are developed fully. The examples and details used support the major points being made.
5	This response answers the question clearly by showing a clear understanding of content and pedagogy. The answer is organized and developed fully. The examples and details used support the major points being made.
4	This response is adequate, it demonstrates an accurate, although limited understanding of content and pedagogy as they relate to the question at hand.
3	This response answers some parts of the question but not others. It shows some understanding of content and pedagogy, but may have a few factual errors. Only some details and examples are provided.
2	This response is unclear, undeveloped, and limited in terms of answering the question. It shows an incomplete understanding of content and pedagogy, and may have many errors.
1	This response doesn't answer the question and shows a deficit in knowledge of content and pedagogy. There are problems with organization of ideas and development of them.
0	This response was left empty, discusses the wrong issue, or can't be read.

Score Reporting

When Will I Receive My Examinee Score Report and in What Form Will It Be?

ETS mails test-score reports six weeks after the test date. There is an exception for computer-based tests and for the Praxis I examinations. Score reports will list your current score and the highest score you have earned on each test you have taken over the last 10 years.

Along with your score report, ETS will provide you with a booklet that offers details on your scores. For each test date, you may request that ETS send a copy of your scores to as many as three score recipients, provided that each institution or agency is eligible to receive the scores.

STUDYING FOR THE TEST

It is critical to your success that you study effectively. Throughout this guide you will find *Praxis Pointers* that will give you tips for successful test taking. The following are a few tips to help get you going:

- Choose a time and place for studying that works best for you. Some people set aside a certain number of hours every morning to study; others may choose to study at night before retiring. Only you know what is most effective for you.
- Use your time wisely and be consistent. Work out a study routine and stick to it; don't let your personal schedule interfere. Remember, seven weeks of studying, is a modest investment to put you on your chosen path.
- Don't cram the night before the test. You may have heard many amazing tales about effective cramming, but don't kid yourself: most of them are false, and the rest are about exceptional people who, by definition, aren't like most of us.
- As you complete the practice test, score your test and thoroughly review the explanations to the questions you answered incorrectly.
- Take notes on material you will want to go over again or research further.

Study Schedule

The following study course schedule allows for thorough preparation to pass the Praxis II Elementary Education 0012. This is a suggested seven-week course of study. However, you can condense this schedule if you are in a time crunch or expand it if you have more time. You may decide to use your weekends for study and preparation and go about your other business during the week. You may even want to record information and listen to your mp3 player or tape as you travel in your car. However you decide to study, be sure to adhere to the structured schedule you devise.

WEEK	ACTIVITY
1	After reading the first chapter to understand the format and content of the exam, begin reading the review sections and take the first practice exam by the end of the week. When you take the practice exam, make sure you simulate real exams conditions.
2	Review your responses to the first practice exam and, using the scoring rubric above, evaluate your answer. Review the appropriate chapter sections. Useful study techniques include highlighting key terms and information, taking notes as you review each section, and putting new terms and information on note cards to help retain the information.
3 and 4	Reread all your note cards, refresh your understanding of the exam's subareas and related skills, review your college textbooks, and read over notes you took in your college classes. This is also the time to consider any other supplementary materials suggested by your counselor or your state education agency.
5	Begin to condense your notes and findings. A structured list of important facts and concepts, based on your note cards, college textbook, course notes, and this book's review chapters will help you thoroughly review for the test.
6	Take the second practice test, adhering to the time limits and simulated test-day conditions, and score your response using the scoring rubric.
7	Review your areas of weakness using all your study materials. This is a good time to retake the practice tests, if time allows.

THE DAY OF THE TEST

Before the Test

- Dress comfortably in layers. You do not want to be distracted by being too hot or too cold while you are taking the test.
- Check your registration ticket to verify your arrival time.
- Plan to arrive at the test center early. This will allow you to collect your thoughts and relax before the test; your early arrival will also spare you the anguish that comes with being late.

- Make sure to bring your admission ticket with you and two forms of identification, one of which must contain a recent photograph, your name, and your signature (e.g., a driver's license). You will not gain entry to the test center without proper identification.

- Bring several sharpened No. 2 pencils with erasers. You will not want to waste time searching for a replacement pencil if you break a pencil. The proctor will not provide pencils or pens at the test center.

- Wear a watch to the test center so you can apportion your testing time wisely. You may not, however, wear one that makes noise or that will otherwise disturb the other test takers.

- Leave all dictionaries, textbooks, notebooks, calculators, briefcases, and packages at home. You may not take these items into the test center.

- Do not eat or drink too much before the test. The proctor will not allow you to make up time you miss if you have to take a bathroom break. You will not be allowed to take materials with you, and you must secure permission before leaving the room.

> *PRAXIS Pointer*
>
> **On the day of the test, be well rested and dress comfortably in layers.**

During the Test

- Pace yourself. ETS administers the Praxis II Elementary Education 0012 in one two-hour sitting with no breaks.

- Follow all of the rules and instructions that the test proctor gives you. Proctors will enforce these procedures to maintain test security. If you do not abide by the regulations, the proctor may dismiss you from the test and notify ETS to cancel your score.

- Listen closely as the test instructor provides the directions for completing the test. Follow the directions carefully.

Take the test! Do your best! Relax! Wait for that passing score to arrive.

REFERENCES

Macdonald, R., and Savin-Baden, M. 2004. *Assessment in Problem-Based Learning*. LTSN Generic Centre Assessment Series, No.7. York: LTSN Generic Centre.

Reading and Language Arts

In preparing for the 0012, you should be aware that there are many wide-ranging "best practices" which allow for good teaching. For example, it is currently accepted that appealing to the different sensory learning modalities (auditory, visual, and tactile/kinesthetic) of students gives them equal access to information. In addition to using a multisensory approach, other general essentials like small class size, small group instruction/cooperative learning, tutoring programs, parent/community involvement, and school-based enrichment programs allow students to engage in a deeper understanding of the content with which they are faced. As the latest research points out, it is most important to support the efforts of the great teacher. As the 2009 Annual Letter from the Bill and Melinda Gates Foundation (BMGF) points out, "It is amazing how big a difference a great teacher makes versus an ineffective one. . . If you want your child to get the best education possible, it is actually more important to get him assigned to a great teacher than to a great school" (BMGF 2009). More than ever, great schools are focusing on exemplary pedagogy, self-reflective teaching, and professional development. Also, a shift has occurred which puts much greater emphasis on student outcomes that can be measured over the delivery of specified programs.

But specifically, when we consider the area of Reading/Language Arts, what are the best practices for teaching reading, writing, and spelling? What do teachers need to know when it comes to theory and practice? What kinds of 0012 test issues arise when one considers curriculum, instruction, and assessment? The following chapter will address many of these important areas as they relate to Reading/Language Arts instruction. We begin with a brief listing of different theoretical approaches to teaching followed by some general approaches to instruction when it comes to elementary education.

THEORY

In order to better understand what teachers do in the classroom, it's important to reflect on different theoretical approaches educators and psychologists have developed over the years. These approaches form the basic foundations for pedagogy in the classroom. Therefore, they are important concepts to know about in your test preparation.

Albert Bandura said that learning occurred by observing others in society. He found that there was a reciprocal relationship between environment and behavior which became more widely known as the social learning theory.

Bloom's Taxonomy: Benjamin Bloom (1956) and a group of educational psychologists developed a six-tiered taxonomy, or classification system, based on intellectual behavior important to the learning process. In ascending order, it consists of *knowledge* (recalling information), *comprehension, application, analysis, synthesis,* and *evaluation.* While all levels of the hierarchy are important, good teaching is partly defined by the degree to which teachers can guide students to think at higher levels of Bloom's Taxonomy; for example, a sixth grade social studies teacher might help students *recall* basic historical facts, *comprehend* a document by writing a summary of its main points, *apply* historical issues or themes to different time periods, *analyze* a document (or an era) for its bias, *synthesize* information from disparate sources and create new conclusions, and *evaluate* the conclusions drawn by scholars about a particular historical phenomenon.

In his theory of constructivism, **Jerome Bruner (1963)** said that learning was an active process whereby students construct new ideas and concepts based upon their current/past experiences and knowledge.

PRAXIS Pointer

Constructed-response tests assess your ability to explain what you know about fundamental concepts in this field.

An early advocate for experiential learning (i.e., learning through experience), **John Dewey** was concerned with how a teacher-centered classroom could negatively impact the classroom environment and learning. He also influenced the progressive movement in education which emphasized problem-solving and the interests and needs of students (Ornstein & Levine 2008).

Differentiated instruction, as explained by Carol Ann Tomilson (2001), is an approach which addresses the diversity of learners in the classroom. Multiple adaptations are made by the teacher to reach individual learners at their own respective stages. As Gregory and Chapman (2002) point out, teachers can differentiate content, assessment, performance tasks, and instructional strategies.

Emergent literacy is Marie Clay's (1966) theory that at the beginning stages of learning to read, the reader develops an association between print and meaning. During this stage of reading development, children engage in retelling familiar stories from memory, using pictures to make predictions, connecting sounds with words, etc.

Emotional Intelligence is Daniel Goleman's (1995) idea that emotional aptitude can be divided into five domains: self-awareness, managing emotions, self-motivation, empathy, and social skills.

Erik Erikson's (1950) psychosocial theory of development delineates what he asserted to be the eight stages of progression toward self-esteem. The eight stages—hope, will, purpose, competence, fidelity, love, caring, and wisdom—begin in infancy and continue throughout one's lifetime.

Experiential learning, which is credited to Dewey, Paolo Friere, and Carl Rogers, among others, says that the teacher must facilitate learning by creating a positive classroom environment in which students are actively engaged (Neil 2005). Moreover, this type of learning is based on the student's experience (through field trips, role plays, etc.).

Howard Gardner (1993), father of the **multiple intelligences theory**, asserts that each person's level of intelligence is a calculus of eight factors: linguistic, musical, logical/mathematical, spatial, bodily/kinesthetic, interpersonal, intrapersonal, and personal.

Lawrence Kohlberg's (1981) theory of moral reasoning suggests that children proceed through a series of stages during which they refine their concept of justice.

Learning styles means that all of us learn through our senses (auditory, visual, and tactile/kinesthetic), and that the teacher should not only teach to a variety of sensory modalities but also assess the learning styles of the individuals in his or her classroom.

Many researchers (David Kolb and Myers-Briggs are examples) have developed inventories that can be used to assess the learning styles of students.

In *All Kinds of Minds*, **Mel Levine (2002)** tries to understand the neurodevelopment of children with learning, developmental, and behavioral problems by recognizing their variations but relying on their strengths in an effort to help them succeed.

Abraham Maslow's (1943) hierarchy of human needs has five stages. The first stage is *physiological and biological needs* (hunger, thirst, and the need for shelter). Only after these fundamental needs have been satisfied can the next stage, *safety needs* (security, protection from physical and emotional harm, health), be addressed. The hierarchy is rounded out by *belonging and love* (family and friends and the feeling of acceptance in relations with others); *esteem* (self respect, autonomy, status, recognition, and attention); and s*elf-actualization* (potential to "become" who you can become and to achieve success in life).

Based on the child development theories of Italian educator Maria Montessori (1870–1952), **Montessori theory (Brehony 2000)** emphasizes self-directed activity on the part of the child and clinical observation on the part of the teacher (often called a *director*, *directress*, or *guide*). Montessori said it was important to adapt the child's learning environment to his or her developmental level. Children make choices in a Montessori classroom, which is often multi-age and characterized by students working independently on different projects. Montessori said it was important to stress physical activity and both gross and fine motor skills when children are absorbing abstract concepts and practical skills. She also stressed that teachers must encourage students to self-correct.

A Swiss psychologist named **Jean Piaget (1955)** constructed a model of child development and learning based on the idea that the developing child builds cognitive structures for understanding his or her environment. He identified four stages of cognitive development. Stage one, the **sensorimotor period** (birth to 2 years), sees the infant move from simple reflexes to conscious behavior. The **preoperational period** (ages 2 to 7) described the child's developing use of symbols. The **concrete operational period** (ages 7 to 11) which is when the child develops logic. The final stage is the **formal operational period** (ages 11 to early adulthood), which is when hypothetical thinking develops. As children move through these different stages of development, they become ready for more challenging cognitive experiences (Ornstein & Levine, 2008).

Originally started after World War II in a small town in Italy in an effort to move forward after Mussolini's reign of fascism, **Reggio Emilia theory** (cited in Caldwell 1997) is an approach to early education which challenges some more traditional conceptions of teacher competence and developmentally appropriate practice. Reggio Emilia teachers assert the importance of "being confused" as contributing to learning, of purposefully allowing mistakes to happen, and of starting a project with no clear sense of where it might end. Other characteristics of this approach are the importance of the child's ability to negotiate in the peer group; the gathering of multiple points of view regarding children's needs, interests, and abilities; and the reliance on parents, teachers, and children to contribute in meaningful ways to the outcome of school experiences. In essence, the teacher creates an atmosphere of community and collaboration that is developmentally appropriate for adults and children alike.

Lev Vygotsky (1978) developed the social cultural learning model. Vygotsky proposed that culture is the prime determinant of individual development, and that language is an important process in the cultural learning scheme. Likewise, children learn when they are in an environment in which they are supported by a more able thinker. **Scaffolding** is a metaphoric term used by Vygotsky to show how parents and teachers can provide temporary assistance to children and students by modeling appropriate behavior or skills. In the classroom, teachers model or demonstrate specific strategies and gradually move the scaffolding away by shifting the responsibility to the student to demonstrate. The scaffold must place the students in the **zone of proximal development**, which is the span between what they can already do independently and what they can do with the guidance of an adult or more able peer.

Grant Wiggins' (1998) concept of "understanding by design" presents a framework for improving student achievement. By emphasizing the teacher's critical role as a designer of student learning, his theory works within the standards-driven curriculum to help teachers clarify learning goals, devise revealing assessments of student understanding, and craft effective and engaging learning activities.

GENERAL APPROACHES TO INSTRUCTION

Cooperative learning is an instructional approach that encourages students to work collaboratively, either as partners or in small groups, on clearly defined tasks. Groups are put together heterogeneously (mixed up) and are rewarded equally for completed tasks. A derivation of cooperative learning is a **jigsaw**, whereby students are grouped to work on a specific task and then redistributed into other groups where they teach their new group members what they worked on in the first group. **Flexible skill groups** are small groups which are formed based on specific goals, activities, and needs. The groups are flexible because children move in and out of them (Opitz 1998).

Constructivism is a framework for instruction based upon the idea that it is important for students to discuss, think, and construct new meaning (Woolfolk 2003). The idea is that students are not just passive receivers of information, but rather that they make meaning from their experiences. According to the theory, students reflect on their experiences and construct an understanding of the world based on those personal experiences. Teachers use this approach when they make learning active, concrete, and important to the lives of their students.

Direct instruction is teacher-centered instruction. It is task-oriented and asks students to learn content and skills through lecture, explicit teaching, direction, and student accountability in a safe and controlled environment (Cruickshank, Jenkins, and Metcalf 2006).

Indirect instruction is another kind of teaching. Here, teachers use brief, on-the-spot mini-lessons as they respond to students' questions or assist students who need specific help. **Mini-lessons** are associated with both direct and indirect instruction. For instance, teachers use direct instruction during the mini-lesson to teach about reading and writing procedures, skills, and strategies, and rely on mini-lessons during a variety of classroom settings: during whole-class activities, in conferences with students, or working with small groups.

Discovery learning is an effort to get students to think for themselves and to promote higher level thinking by asking questions and creating activities that promote the discovery of information a teacher wants the student to understand. For instance, to encourage students to learn about secondary colors, a teacher might ask some questions and then give students primary colors and the directions to mix those colors however they see fit and note their observations (Cruickshank, Jenkins, and Metcalf 2006).

Experiential learning (Neil 2005) is learning from direct experience. It is hands-on "learning by doing." Students do this when they go on field trips, participate in role plays, etc.

"I" messages. Whenever a teacher can, he or she should use "I" messages ("I wasn't sure what you were saying here," as opposed to "This is unclear" or "You didn't say that here." Why? Because the "I" type of message makes the student less defensive and more reflective on his or her work.

Independent study includes activities where students work by themselves to understand material. This may include journals, learning logs, or assigned questions. Independent study encourages independence, responsibility, autonomy, and metacognition (Williams 2003).

Interactive instruction relies heavily on discussion and sharing among participants. Seaman and Fellenz (1989) suggest that discussion and sharing provide learners with opportunities to not only interact with the teacher's ideas but also to devise a variety of approaches that differ from those of other students in the class. Thus, students can learn from peers and teachers to develop social skills and abilities, to organize their thoughts, and to develop arguments.

Learning centers are multi-level stations where activities designed for specific instructional purposes provide reinforcement, independent practice, and discovery. In a kindergarten program, these are areas that contain materials (blocks, pretend household items, art supplies, etc.) where children can explore their own interests at their own pace.

> **PRAXIS Pointer**
>
> Take your time to answer all parts of the question clearly and organize your answer coherently. List each element of the question that you must address in your response.

Mastery learning is Benjamin Bloom's (1980) idea that all children can learn when provided with the appropriate learning conditions in the classroom. They may not all learn at the same rate, but they can all succeed when the information is broken down into sequences (Ornstein & Levine 2008). In this approach, children do not advance until they have mastered the level of understanding with which they are presented.

Problem-based learning gives students open-ended and challenging problems that require investigation, collaboration, and solutions (Lambros 2002). Problem-based learning allows students to generate solutions in a collaborative venue.

Reteaching is used when students don't get it the first time around and the teacher must consider learning styles, multiple intelligences, small group instruction, cooperative learning, in-class writing, and other methods to accomplish the unfulfilled learning goals.

Scaffolding is a metaphoric term used by Vygotsky (1978) to show how parents and teachers can provide temporary assistance to children and students by modeling appropriate behavior or skills. In the classroom, teachers model or demonstrate specific strategies and gradually shift the responsibility to the student who must ultimately display mastery of the learning goal.

Student-centered classroom posits that students are best served in a student-centered classroom, rather than in a teacher-centered classroom. In this setting, teachers function as coaches rather than leaders, and they encourage students in a variety of ways. On the other hand, a **teacher-centered classroom** assumes that students are passive recipients of knowledge. On the plus side, teachers stay in control and help students learn self-discipline, responsibility, cooperation, and problem-solving skills (Tompkins 2002).

Think-pair-share means think about your answer (individually), turn to your partner and talk about what you think, and then share with the larger group what you think about the issue or topic.

CURRICULUM

When one considers curriculum and its role in preparing for the 0012 test, the first thought that comes to mind is the notion of standards: there are state curricular standards that teachers must understand and adhere to. Teachers must construct units with lessons that conform to these standards and are sequenced in an effort to achieve standardized goals. The curriculum committees of school districts study the standards and communicate them to the schools, which in turn provide guidelines and resources to teachers. In terms of the curriculum, teachers have goals and objectives that they must follow. The goals must be measurable, and they must be assessed in a variety of ways. Teachers must write objectives that are, as Bloom (1978) indicated, *cognitive* (thinking), *affective* (emotions), and *psychomotor* (physical skills). A teacher might write an objective like, "After my lesson, students will be able to add equivalent forms of whole numbers (e.g., $5 + 10 = 7 + 8$). Additionally, students will be able to represent equivalent forms through the use of symbols. This will be assessed by having students construct and solve ten equations." In the cognitive domain, teachers should make students strive for higher levels of Bloom's Taxonomy in order to become better critical thinkers. Likewise, students should become more aware of their own cognitive processes (**metacognitive**). Teachers should strive to reach their ideal outcomes by **back-planning** (thinking first about outcomes they want to achieve and then creating units, weekly plans, and daily lessons that will lead to those goals).

Overall, the structure in curricular design usually follows:

goals (state/national standards)—for instance "Understand various rock formations."

concepts—big understandings—"The earth changes over time."

content—the subject areas being developed expressed in nouns—"Volcanoes"

skills—what students will be able to do expressed in verbs—"Locate a volcano and analyze its stages."

Beyond these broad objectives, what specific areas of curriculum are important when it comes to Reading and Language Arts? Generally speaking, teachers should employ a program of **balanced literacy**, which aims to achieve a balance between listening, speaking, reading, and writing programs within the classroom, while also maintaining a mixture of whole language and phonics approaches. It is always good pedagogy to use a balanced approach in a language arts classroom. But what else is important? The following is a series of strategies, organized under several broad categories within Reading and Language Arts: Teaching Word Recognition and Language Acquisition, Teaching Reading, Teaching Writing, Teaching Spelling, and Assessment for the Language Arts. These lists are meant to be starting points. They are by no means exhaustive, and in fact should encourage you to look further for a deeper understanding of these concepts in an effort to most effectively answer the essay questions on the 0012 test.

TEACHING WORD RECOGNITION AND LANGUAGE ACQUISITION

Affixes are attachments to the ends or beginnings of the roots of words. An affix that is "fixed to" the beginning of a word is called a **prefix**; one that is fixed to the ending of a word is called a **suffix**. For example, the word *anthropology* has two affixes, a prefix (*anthro-*, "man") and a suffix (*-logy*, "a theory or science"). The word *paternal* has the Latin **root** *pater* ("father"), which is affixed by the suffix *-nal* ("one who acts like"). Teachers must show students how to attach prefixes to the beginnings of words and how to attach suffixes to the ends of words.

Antonyms are words with opposite meanings.

Decoding is the process students use to sound out written words they do not recognize. For instance, if *hike* isn't immediately recognized, the student may identify the *h* sound, the *k* sound, the long vowel *i* sound, and then blend these sounds together (Graves, Juel, & Graves, 1998).

Digraphs are two letters that represent one speech sound, for instance *sh* in *shoe*, *ch* in *chip*, or *ng* in *bring*.

Diphthongs are two-vowel combinations where both vowels are heard, but not quite making their usual sounds because of the blending, for instance *ou* in *doubt*.

Homographs are words that are spelled alike but have different meanings (*plane* as in airplane versus *plane* as in geometry).

Idioms are words that are particular to a specific language. An example of an idiomatic expression is "chill out," which means "relax" and not, as literal interpretation would suggest, "get really cold."

Initial Blends are when two or more consonant sounds are joined, such as *tr* in *track*, or the joining of the first consonant and vowel sounds in a word, such as *c* and *a* in *cat*. This skill is important in learning phonics.

Lexeme refers to a word unit that corresponds to a set of forms taken by a single word. For example, the lexeme *swim* has a present form (*swims*), a past form (*swam*), and a participle form (*swimming*).

Morphemes are the smallest meaningful units in language, word parts that can change the meaning of a word. A morpheme can't necessarily stand alone as a word. For instance, the word *untreatable* has three morphemes: *un, treat,* and *able*.

Phonemes are sound units of speech that are the component parts of spoken language. Phonemes are the smallest units of sound that can change the meanings of spoken words. For example, if you change the first phoneme in *rat* from *r* to *h*, the word *rat* changes to *hat*. The English language has 44 phonemes. A few words, such as *a* or *oh*, have only one phoneme. Most words have more than one phoneme. **Phonemic awareness** means teaching students that words are made up of sounds. Recognizing that sounds combine to create words, understanding rhymes, and seeing that words can be broken into syllables all indicate phonemic awareness.

Phonogram refers to a succession of letters representing the same phonological unit in different words, such as *ed* in *led, red,* and *bed*.

Phonological systems are important in both oral and written language. There are 26 letters and 44 sounds and many ways to combine the letters—particularly the vowels—to spell these sounds. Sounds are called **phonemes**. When these letter combinations are represented in print, they are called **graphemes**.

Phonics is a way of teaching reading and spelling that stresses basic symbol-sound relationships as a way to decode words in beginning instruction. Phonics lets us know that there is a connection between sounds (phonemes) and letters (graphemes). It is said that systematic and explicit instruction in phonics improves word recognition, spelling, and reading comprehension. Phonics helps when it comes to breaking down words into sounds so that students can see how sounds form into words. Phonics is recommended for students in K-2.

Syllabication is the division of words into syllables.

Syntactic system is the structural, or grammatical, organization of English that regulates how words are combined into sentences. Many of the capitalization and punctuation rules that elementary students learn in forming simple, compound, and complex sentences reflect the syntactic system of language.

TEACHING READING

Context clues are hints within the text about the meaning of a word.

Developmentally appropriate practices for reading instruction. Preschool teachers share books, talk about letters, and create literacy-rich environments. School-age students move through other stages. In kindergarten, they are read to and begin to see relationships between words and print. In first grade, they retell stories, read aloud, and write stories. These practices are developmentally appropriate, given the level of the student.

Fluency teaches students to read accurately and quickly, and to connect word recognition with comprehension. Students also often connect the book to their world. While less fluent readers try to decode individual words at the expense of the bigger picture, fluent readers read with greater speed and accuracy. Fluency develops in many ways: teachers model it with effortless and expressive reading; students reread the same text on multiple occasions, giving them ample opportunity to improve in their fluency; the teacher encourages parents to read to their children aloud at home; and students listen to books on tape or CD.

A teacher might assess fluency by listening to oral reading: Does it have expression? Are readers pausing in correct places and putting emphasis on the right words? To assess fluency, the teacher could select a passage at grade level, ask a student to read it aloud for one minute, count the number of words read, keep track of errors, subtract errors from total words read, and then graph this over time. The student has a problem in fluency if he or she reads and makes more than 10 percent word-recognition errors, can't read aloud with expression, or demonstrates poor comprehension.

Reader readiness is when children show signs that they are getting ready to read. For example, they may pretend they are reading by holding the book the right way and turning pages. They may understand how the book works, with lines read from left to right, from top to bottom of the page. They may discuss the story and relate it to their own ideas and experiences, or they may retell the story. Although children can't read yet, they may know the correlations between letters and sound, and can recognize letters and their own names. They have an interest in books and also in writing.

Sight word is a word that is easily recognized as a whole and does not require word analysis for identification or pronunciation (Dolch p. 220, Sight Vocabulary List).

Scope and sequence of skills is a report that the teacher follows which tells him or her what skills the student needs to progress to the next functional level and what activities need to be completed in order to reach those goals.

Whole language is an approach to reading instruction focusing on reading for meaning and the integration of the four aspects of language: reading, writing, listening, and speaking. Often, teachers use trade books as opposed to basal readers, and teach phonics and other skills in the context of the reading.

Visual literacy involves teaching students skills like evaluating an advertisement, a website, or information from the Internet.

Writing—when a teacher is teaching reading, there is always a connection that needs to be made to writing—students write to access content; to think before, during, and after the reading process.

Stages of literacy are, in sequential order, *emergent, developing,* and *transitional.*

Emergent literacy describes the period from birth–5 years, when literacy develops gradually as the child changes from a non-reader to a beginning reader. Certain factors contribute to emergent literacy, such as:

- Knowing the parts of the book
- Knowing the directionality of print (left to right)
- Understanding how voice and print match up
- Sight vocabulary
- Phonemic awareness (an understanding that the spoken word is the printed word)
- Knowing the alphabet
- Being able to socially interact with peers and adults
- Being exposed to frequent experiences with print
- Accessing schema (prior knowledge)
- Being motivated
- Having fluency (being able to speak the words)

Teachers can support emergent literacy by making sure the book is developmentally and age-appropriate and by using a variety of approaches, including:

- Direct instruction—give students the task
- Partner reading—partners sit together and take turns reading
- Word Wall—an organized and displayed group of words in the class
- Shared reading—adult reading aloud to student
- Repeated readings—same book, more than once
- Reader response—ask questions
- Text innovation—kids rewrite story (with a new ending, a new problem, etc.)
- Shared writing (publishing)
- Language experience approach (LEA)—I write or talk about what I experience, then read it

Developing literacy, from mid-first to late second grade, sees the student becoming more independent in reading.

Transitional literacy is the period from second grade and beyond. Now, students work with independent level materials.

Types of Reading

Basal readers are anthologies used to teach elementary age children developmentally appropriate texts (short stories, excerpts from narratives, etc.). **Trade books** are whole books that have been published and approved for teaching elementary students.

Children's literature is an umbrella phrase for the books that children read. Teachers use a variety of criteria in selecting a text for children, including:

- Repeated refrain (for kindergarten)
- Interest
- Age/level
- Do they need to see pictures?
- Does it balance the curriculum?

There are different genres of children's literature, many of which are mentioned by Anderson (2006). These include:

- Novel
- Short story
- Science fiction
- Parable—"The Good Samaritan"
- Fable—has a moral, has animals, Aesop, "The Fox and the Grapes"
- Myth—Greek, Roman, Native American
- Legend—exaggerated stories about real people
- Folk tale—oral tradition
- Play
- Mystery
- Historical fiction
- Adventure story—part made up, part based on real events
- Fantasy—set in an imaginary world with imaginary characters
- Poetry

Certain **literary devices** are used in children's literature, such as:

Plot: What are the elements of plot?
- Rising action
- Internal/external conflict
- Complication
- Suspense
- Crisis
- Climax/turning point
- Resolution

Point of View: First person, second person, third person objective, third person omniscient

Setting: Where the story takes place

Characterization: The people in the story. We learn about characters based on their words, thoughts, appearances, etc.

Dialogue: What characters say to each other

Foreshadowing: Hints that let you predict what will happen next

Figurative language
- Metaphor: comparison using the verb *to be*—my love is a red rose
- Simile: comparison using *like/as*—my love is like a red rose
- Hyperbole: over-exaggeration (Example: I ate as much as a horse.)
- Personification: give human attributes to non-human things (Example: fear clutched me.)

Symbolism: something stands for something else

Imagery: appeals to senses

Tone: feeling or emotion of the piece

Theme: main idea

Word choice

Mechanics

Dialect: use of slang or regional language

With respect to poetry, there are many different types of poems:

Lyrical: like a song

Concrete: a visual poem

Free verse: no regular rhyme scheme

Narrative: tells a story

Couplet: a pair of lines that have similar rhythm and rhyme

Elegy: sad poem honoring a deceased person

Sonnet: 14 lines; rhymes in a specific pattern

Limerick: five lines; humorous

Haiku: three lines, 5/7/5 syllables

Similarly, there are devices that are specific to poems:

Verse: a line of a poem

Meter: the rhythm made by stressed and unstressed syllables

- Example: "Do not go gentle into that good night" by Dylan Thomas has a rising meter known as iambic pentameter

Stanza: a paragraph of a poem

Rhyme and sound patterns

- Rhyme scheme: ABABCDCDEFEFGG (English sonnet)
- Onomatopoeia: a word imitates the sound it represents ("splash," "hiss," "meow," or "buzz")
- Alliteration: repeated consonant sounds ("Fly away, my feathered friend.")
- Assonance: repeated vowel sound (burlap, sack, lap)

Imagery: pictures created by words that appeal to the senses

Likewise, there are various types of non-fiction:

Biography: story of a person by another person

Autobiography: story of an author's life

Essay: one non-fiction point of view

News article: details who, what, when, where, why, and how

Editorial: opinion

Professional journal article

Book on a research topic

Book review

Political speech

Technical manual: how to

Primary source material: diary

In terms of non-fiction, there are certain questions the teacher should ask about the passage:

What's the purpose? To persuade, inform, analyze, evaluate?
What does the author appeal to? Reason (facts)—logos, emotion
    (feelings)—pathos, authority (source material and its reputation)—ethos?
How is it organized?

How are **reading levels** determined? Books are geared toward specific age groups and abilities. On the back cover of some trade books you might see "RL 4.8," which means the reading level is for a fourth grade student in her eighth month. Some publishers have a grade level on the front cover, while other companies have websites listing leveled books. Districts also maintain lists of leveled books. While many publishers have their own methods of leveling books, one commonly known approach is the **Fry Readability Graph**, which allows teachers to measure the reading level of a text by randomly selecting three 100-word passages from a book or an article and plotting the average number of syllables and the average number of sentences per 100 words on the graph to determine the grade level of the material.

Pre-Reading Activities

Pre-reading activities get students ready to read. They help students become motivated by relating the reading to their everyday lives.

Schemata is the term for what the student already knows. It is important to activate that prior knowledge and use it in the current reading process. A commonly known method to activate schemata is **KWL**, in which the teacher asks the student to understand what I *know*, what I *want* to learn, and what I *learned*.

SQ3R is a method students can use prior to reading. They are approaching a book by surveying, asking questions, and reading, reciting, and reviewing.

Vocabulary can be introduced and taught prior to reading a story. Similarly, **concepts** or ideas in the story can be explained prior to reading.

While Reading

Choral reading has two or more individuals reading aloud from the same text in unison to enhance oral reading fluency.

Echo reading is a strategy in which the teacher reads a line or passage with good expression, and then calls on students to read it back. This is a good technique to use with emergent readers to help them build reading fluency.

Partner reading asks a student and a partner to take turns reading aloud to each other.

Reading to students is a traditional method where students can hear texts spoken. This is particularly effective where students are non-native speakers of English.

Reciprocal reading, also known as reciprocal teaching, is a set of four strategies the teacher can use with struggling readers to help them develop comprehension. In pairs or small groups, the students take turns "playing teacher" in activities in which they question, summarize, clarify, and predict.

> **PRAXIS Pointer**
>
> Understand the scoring criteria for the exam. Ask someone else to read your practice tests and have them apply the scoring rubric found in this book.

Oral reading by students is when they read aloud to increase fluency. This is particularly effective when teaching drama or when reading dialogue.

Shared reading is an activity in which the teacher and students sit together around a text so that all can listen, see the printed words, and look at the pictures. Individual students are selected to point to the printed word and the other students join in, reading at their own level of expertise. Sometimes, the teacher reads a passage while pointing to the words to help young readers learn to read.

SSR is sustained silent reading. As **Fitzgerald and Graves** (2004) assert, elementary teachers are preparing students to become lifelong readers, and most of that reading (in the upper grades and beyond) will be done in silence. Therefore, silent reading should be encouraged in school and at home. A well-known SSR program is Drop Everything And Read, known as DEAR.

Graphic organizers are cognitive maps and other visual representations that help students organize and understand information in a story.

Guided reading is a strategy by which the teacher provides structure via modeling strategies in order to move beginning readers towards independence. While the reading process is going on, the teacher encourages the student to make notes about concepts, answer questions they may have come up with in pre-reading, reread confusing passages, look closely at unfamiliar vocabulary and its context, etc.

Language Experience Approach (LEA) is a method of teaching reading which is dictated by the reader's own language and experience. This approach allows the reader to read words common to his or her environment. LEA usually starts with a shared class experience. For instance, the class goes to an assembly on reptiles, and after it, the teacher asks the students to dictate the story of the experience as the teacher writes what they say word for word on a large piece of paper or PowerPoint slide. The teacher reads the sentences back to the class, finalizes the story, and then has the class read it over. It is exciting for students to read their own words; moreover, they are building their vocabularies. From this point on, the teacher can focus the lesson on concepts that need further reinforcement.

Literature circles are important to the cooperative reading process. Tompkins (2002) endorsed four components of literature circles: reading, responding, creating projects, and sharing.

Visualizing means picturing in your mind what is happening in the text to increase comprehension.

Post-Reading

After the reading is completed, there are many activities the teacher can implement to assess comprehension. The teacher can **ask questions** that ask students to draw inferences or find important ideas. The teacher can lead a **discussion**. Students can **draw a graphic or illustrated example from the text** which can be a helpful tactile, kinesthetic, and artistic approach to understanding a story. Similarly, students can make **graphic organizers or concept maps** about the main ideas and supporting details in the story. Finally, they can **act out the text**.

Post-reading activities encourage students to reflect on what they have read. They can do this by writing answers to comprehension and interpretation questions, journaling, summarizing, and rewriting information.

General Methods for Teaching Reading

Repeated readings mean that the student reads the same passage several times while getting guidance from the teacher. **Oral readings** are reinforced through audio-tapes and tutors.

Independent reading is when students read on their own. Examples that were previously mentioned:

SSR (sustained silent reading)
DEAR (Drop Everything And Read)

Phonics teaches students the relationship between letters and sounds.

Sight word recognition stresses the high-frequency words (*a, an, the, is, to, are,* and *can*) which are so well-known that they can be read instantly. By teaching these words to early readers, they have a set of words they know, which gives them the opportunity to focus their attention on words they may have more trouble figuring out.

Whole language is a big-picture approach to reading. In contrast with the more skill-based instruction of **phonics** (where students sound out letters and sounds in words), and the more traditional approach of **sight reading** (where students get to look at and say words), proponents of **whole language** say that reading is a transactional process whereby the student makes meaning within his or her context, is immersed in a richly textual environment, chooses texts to read, interprets texts, writes (using invented spelling), and publishes.

Many educators suggest using a **balanced approach** between these three methodologies.

Decoding is the capacity for the student to apply his or her knowledge of letter-sound relationships and letter patterns to correctly pronounce written words.

Structural analysis means breaking words into parts or syllables, which is said to give students word-attack skills to tackle new words. In other words, by understanding the structure or parts of words, it will help them to decode new words in the future. For example:

v/cv open – v = vowel (o) c = consonant (p) v = vowel (e)

vc/cv winter ("inte" in winter is vowel, consonant, consonant, vowel)

Context clues are ascertained when the reader uses prediction to figure out what a word might mean. **Syntactic cues** include grammar, word order, and word endings.

Semantics is the study of meaning in communication. When one studies semantics, one considers words and their **denotations**, or dictionary definitions, and **connotations**, or emotional associations. Semantics can provide hints to readers for meaning.

Homonyms are words that sound the same but are spelled differently. (to/two/too)

Antonyms are words that have opposite meanings. (hot/cold)

Synonyms are different words with similar meanings. (car/auto)

Phonemes are the individual sounds in words.

Graphemes are the written letters in words.

Reading workshops are designed to encourage students to read self-selected books independently or in small groups. Afterwards, students are expected to respond to the books by writing in their reading logs and discussing the book in small groups with other students who are reading the same book. This approach helps students to become fluent readers and to deepen their appreciation of books and reading.

In general, **good readers** use a variety of strategies. For instance, they use **metacognition** (they know their knowing and think about their thinking). Before reading, good readers clarify their purpose, preview the text, annotate, adjust purpose with pace, check their comprehension, use graphic organizers and cognitive maps, ask and answer questions as they read, summarize big ideas, "think aloud," predict what might happen next, summarize what they have learned, and connect what they have read to other ideas and concepts. **Good reading teachers** help students access prior knowledge and form mental images as they read. These teachers realize that learning to read begins prior to school. They use a variety of materials, approaches, and texts to ensure success. They differentiate instruction according to their students' unique abilities and challenges. Further, they provide personal attention to students.

TEACHING WRITING

Tompkins (2002) points out that there is a distinction between drawing and writing. Developing writers first learn how to form letters and the direction of writing on a page. As they begin to match letters and sounds, they start to see that the words they put on the page have meaning and can tell a story. When students begin to master composition at this level, teachers further encourage their progress in writing by modeling, conferencing, using peer review, and other methods. The following section will explain different techniques teachers can use when teaching writing.

Conferencing is a chance for a teacher to give individualized feedback to the student on his or her writing. It is a valuable tool when a student has the opportunity to revise. Teacher and student should sit side-by-side and look at the paper together. You can read the paper aloud or ask the student to do so; ideally, the student will hear parts of the paper that don't sound correct. The teacher should focus on a few areas by asking questions; he or she should also look for patterns of significant error in the writing as opposed to overwhelming the student with numerous errors.

Four-square writing asks student to brainstorm a topic by making a list, and then fill in a chart like this:

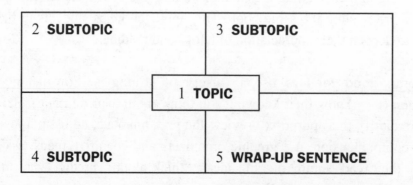

Topic: student writes it in the center of the box.

Subtopics: the teacher encourages the student to use the square to add details and examples.

Wrap-up sentence includes the ideas from all four squares.

For instance, if a student is writing a topic on her favorite food, pizza:

1. Pizza is my favorite food.
2. It tastes great.
3. It's fun to eat.
4. It's hot.
5. My favorite food is pizza because it tastes great, it's fun to eat, and it's hot.

Guided writing is the idea that the classroom teacher supports student development with the writing process. Students are required to write sentences or passages while the teacher guides the process and instruction through conferences and mini-lessons.

In **interactive writing**, teachers and students compose passages and stories that are written collaboratively. Students are free to print some words or interact with the print as facilitated by teacher, for example, with a shared pen.

Journal writing is a great way to get students to practice writing, especially if you use high-interest prompts (Would you like to have an identical twin? What time should your bedtime be and why? What happened to you this weekend?)

Orthography is the study of symbols in a writing system; it also refers to correct or standardized spelling according to established usage in a given language.

Peer editing/peer review. Students work with a peer—usually someone in the same class—to help improve, revise, and edit a piece of their own writing.

Praise/Question/Polish is a revising strategy in which the reader finds something to praise, something that needs more explaining, and something to improve upon:

PRAISE: Find at least one thing (and preferably more) praise-worthy about the paper. Was it well-written? Was it logical and on subject? Were there parts of the paper that resonated with you? Was there something memorable? Did it help put things in a different perspective for you? Did it cause an epiphany for you?

QUESTION: Point out at least one thing in the paper about which you may have a question. Was there a point in need of clarification? Was there need to better explain an idea or give examples?

POLISH: Point out at least one thing that could make the paper better. The teacher should model how this is done in a constructive manner.

In this process, the peer editor also reads the paper for grammatical and mechanical errors before returning it to the student and ultimately the teacher.

Portfolio assessment provides a body of student work—essentially, a portfolio—that can be used to evaluate writing development over a longer period of time.

Resource/reference materials. The teacher should be familiar with different types of reference works (dictionary, thesaurus, atlas, almanac, encyclopedia, Internet searches), as well as other sources like books, journal articles, newspaper and magazine articles, primary vs. secondary sources, etc. The teacher should show students how to use different types of resources for different research questions.

Example: For a project about the painting techniques of Henri Matisse for fifth grade students, what are the top three kinds of resources you would recommend to the students and why?

How would you encourage those same students to research a sit-in that happened in your town twenty years ago?

Researching and writing: The teacher should let students know about the three ways they can take notes: quoting, paraphrasing, or summarizing a source. The teacher should also be able to expose a student to citations and bibliographies.

Rubric is a set of scoring guidelines for assessing student work including a summary listing of the characteristics that distinguish high-quality work from low-quality assignments.

Stages of writing development:

PRAXIS Pointer

Time yourself when you take the practice tests. Take the practice tests under the same conditions you will take the actual tests.

Undifferentiated/pre-writing (ages 3–5) — random marks on paper

Differentiated (approximately age 4) If the sentence reads, "The sky was dark" and the student writes a heavier mark for the word "dark."

Picture writing/pictographic (ages 4–6)—student draws only

Scribble writing—student attempts to write, knows words represent thoughts

Random letter—student knows letters represent sounds

Invented spelling (K-1)—students attempt to "sound it out" I luv mom."

Conventional writing—"You will pass the Praxis."

At what writing stage are each of the following students?

My Bruthor Jon cam to play with me he playd Socer
    Invented spelling
ARtLS
    Random letter

Stages of the writing process:

Pre-writing—the initial creative stage of writing, prior to drafting, in which the writer formulates ideas, gathers information, organizes or plans. This can happen through brainstorming, clustering, outlining, and webbing/cognitive mapping.

Drafting—writing a first draft, keeping in mind knowledge of audience.

Revising—adding, deleting, substituting, or moving around information in large or small ways.

Editing—proofreading done with the teacher's guidance for sentence level errors in grammar, mechanics, spelling, and punctuation. Spell check and grammar check on the computer can be helpful in this process.

Publishing—Once students make improvements to a draft, the teacher makes the writing public by sharing it and distributing it to the class, school, or parents.

Author's Chair is a special chair set up in the class where students, at the end of the writing process, can present their work and get feedback. According to Rief and Heimburge (2006), this program moves from full teacher ownership to student ownership.

It is important to note that the process is **recursive**, meaning it goes back and forth from stage to stage in a sometimes non-sequential order. For instance, a student could be drafting and realize he or she needs to make a change, so he or she would go back to the pre-writing stage and do some freewriting on the topic.

TEACHING SPELLING

Generally speaking, spelling instruction has evolved from the traditional "list" assigned at the beginning of the week and assessed on Friday. Methods employed now include having students study the parts of words, break them down, sort them, use them in sentences, and, finally, testing them on the words. The following section highlights important concepts when it comes to teaching spelling.

Emergent spelling is typical of preschoolers, ages 3–5, and involves the stringing and scribbling of letters to form words. Children may write from left to right, right to left, top to bottom, or randomly across the page. Although students tend to use both upper- and lowercase letters, they often prefer using uppercase letters. This is the period when students learn **invented spelling**, a technique used by beginning writers to spell words using whatever knowledge of sounds or visual patterns they can access, before formal spelling strategy is learned.

Letter name spelling is common to students 5–7 years of age. At this point, students learn to represent phonemes in words with letters. This shows that they have a rudimentary understanding of the alphabetic principle, understanding that a link exists between letters and sounds.

Within-word spelling is common in the 7–9 age group. Students understand the alphabetic principle and they learn how to spell long-vowel patterns and r-controlled vowels. Examples of within-word spelling include *liev* (live), *sope* (soap), *huose* (house), and *bern* (burn). Students experiment with long-vowel patterns and learn that words such as *come* and *bread* are exceptions that do not fit the vowel patterns. Sometimes, students tend to confuse spelling patterns and spell meet as *mete*, and they also tend to reverse the order of letters, such as *form* for from and *gril* for girl.

Derivational relations spelling is common among students ages 11–14. Here, students explore the relationship between spelling and meaning, and learn that words with related meanings are often related in spelling, despite changes in vowel and consonant sounds (e.g., *wise-wisdom, sign-signal, nation-national*). Examples of spelling errors include*: critisize* (criticize), *appearence* (appearance), and *committe* (committee). The focus in this stage is on morphemes, and students learn about Greek and Latin root words and affixes. They also begin to examine etymologies and the role of history in shaping how words are spelled. They learn about eponyms (words from people's names), such as *maverick* and *sandwich*.

Conventional spelling is the final stage, when standard spelling is the correct form for written documents.

Stages of spelling development (Gentry 1981)

> *Random letter*
> *Pre-phonetic* (uses some letters correctly)
> *Early phonetic* (might get A at the beginning)
> *Phonetic* (student spells words the way they sound)
> *Transitional* (mixture of correct and phonetic spelling)
> *Correct*

At what stage are these students, in terms of their spelling?

> *Sry* (for fish), *lvn* (for bend)
>   Random letter
> *Fss* (for fish), *nd (for bend)*
>   Letter name
> *Sailer* (for sailor), *flatt* (for flat)
>   transitional

Some basic **rules for spelling** include:

> *i* before *e* (ex. *lie*) except after *c* (ex. *receipt*), or when sounding like *a* as in *neighbor* and *weigh* (ex. *vein*).

> If a word ends in silent *e*, drop the *e* before adding the suffix (*skate/skating*), unless the suffix begins with a consonant (*skate/skateboard*).

> If a word ends in a consonant and *y* (*worry*) change *y* to *i* before adding a suffix (*worried*); if a word ends in a vowel and *y* (*play*) keep the *y* and add suffix (*playing*).

> Double the final consonant before adding the suffix if a one-syllable word ends with a consonant preceded by a vowel (*tan/tanned*).

ASSESSMENT FOR THE LANGUAGE ARTS

Obviously, assessments give students the opportunity to understand what they have learned, and they give teachers the chance to reflect on their methods and change approaches for the future. In other words, assessments help both teachers and students to understand what they know and don't know and to evaluate what needs to be done to ensure the learning goals. The following section briefly describes the different types of assessments a language arts teacher can use. Again, it is by no means exhaustive and will hopefully encourage you to pursue further study in this important area.

Authentic assessment is a technique to examine students' collective abilities via real-world challenges that requires them to apply their relevant skills and knowledge.

Formal assessments are traditional forms which include quizzes, tests (which, if planned well, help teachers and students see how they are doing), projects, papers, portfolios, group essays, and standardized tests.

Formative evaluation is ongoing evaluation during an instructional sequence to allow for alteration and improvement on the part of the student. It helps engage students in the ongoing assessment of their progress through methods like observations, asking questions, self and peer assessments, etc.

Informal assessment is, as the name indicates, less "formal" than the traditional forms of assessment. With respect to language arts, the teacher can do an **informal reading inventory**, whereby the student reads a passage out loud and the teacher evaluates his or her reading at first for fluency and, later, through questions, for comprehension. The teacher listens to the student read and then analyzes what the student did wrong. Errors may include inserting, deleting, omitting, or substituting words. Another kind of informal assessment is a **running record**, whereby the teacher has the student read a new passage at his or her level and keeps a record of mispronounced, omitted, or repeated words. Then, the teacher analyzes it (which is called a **miscue analysis**) to look for patterns (say, where the student self-corrected or made an error) and see how to help. A full description of this assessment can be found at www.readinga-z.com/guided/runrecord.html.

Cloze procedure is another kind of informal assessment; in this case, the student is given a reading passage where words are deleted and he or she has to complete the blank spaces.

An **anecdotal record** is an informal account made by the teacher of the child's day. In retelling, the teacher asks the student to retell the story, perhaps by looking at a graphic organizer or notes.

Journals are informal assessment sites where students regularly write down their thoughts, experiences, and responses to readings.

Performance-based assessment asks students to perform a task. For example, a student may be asked to give a speech about certain historical events, generate scientific hypotheses, solve math problems, converse in a foreign language, or conduct research on an assigned topic. The teacher then assesses the quality of the student's work based on rubric.

A **portfolio** is a collection of the student's work over time which, ideally, demonstrates progress.

Reading logs are a form of journaling whereby students write about what they read. This writing may address characters, inferences, plot, etc.

Reflective teaching involves the ability to make changes in the classroom based on research, analysis, and reflection upon one's practice. Often, teachers will keep a journal in which they record their reflective observations of their practice in an effort to improve.

Summative evaluation is an evaluation that comes at the conclusion of an educational program or instructional sequence. It measures learning as it relates to content standards and creates a benchmark. In this type of assessment, state and district tests as well as unit and chapter tests are used to see how effectively a classroom or program is performing.

REFERENCES

Anderson, N. 2006. *Elementary Children's Literature*. Boston: Pearson Education.

"The Art of Peer Review: Praise, Question, Polish." Retrieved January 9, 2009, from http://coefaculty.valdosta.edu/stgrubbs/The%20Art%20of%20Peer%20Review.htm.

The Bill and Melinda Gates Foundation. 2009. *2009 Annual letter from Bill Gates: U.S. Education.* Retrieved 2/6/09 from www.gatesfoundation.org/annual-letter/Pages/2009-united-states-education.aspx

Bloom, B.S. 1956. *Taxonomy of Educational Objectives: The classification of educational goals. New York: McKay.*

———. 1980. *All our children learning*. New York: McGraw-Hill.

Brehony, K. (2000). Montessori, individual work in the elementary school classroom. *History of Education*, 29, 115–128.

Bruner, J. 1963. *Acts of meaning*. Cambridge, MA: Harvard UP.

Caldwell, L.B. 1997. *Bringing Reggio Emilia Home: An Innovative Approach to Early Childhood Education*. New York: Teacher's College.

Clark, D. R. 2004. Instructional System Design Concept Map. Retrieved September 30, 2007, from http://nwlink.com/~donclark/hrd/ahold/isd.html.

Clay, M.M. 1966. "Emergent Reading Behavior." PhD dissertation, Univ. of Aukland, New Zealand.

Cruickshand, D.R., Jenkins, D.B., and Metcalf, K.K. [DNS: date] *The Act of Teaching*. Boston: McGraw-Hill.

Dolch, Edward William. 1948. *Problems in Reading*. Illinois: The Gerard Press.

Erickson, E. 1950. *Childhood and society*. New York: Norton.

Fitzgerald, J. and Graves, M.F. 2004. *Scaffolding Reading Experiences for English-Language Learners*. Norwood, MA: Christopher-Gordon.

Fry, Edward. 1977. *Elementary Reading Instruction*. New York: McGraw-Hill.

Gardner, H. 1993. *Frames of Mind: The Theory of Multiple Intelligences*. Basic Books.

Gentry, J.R. 1981. Learning to spell developmentally. *Reading Teacher*, 34: 378381.

Graves, M.F., Juel, C., and Graves, B.B. 1998. *Teaching Reading in the 21st Century*. Boston: Allyn and Bacon.

Gregory, G.H. and Chapman, C. 2002. *Differentiated Instructional Strategies*. Thousand Oaks, CA: Corwin Press.

Goleman, D. 1995. *Emotional Intelligence*. New York: Bantam.

Instructional Strategies Online. Dec. 27, 2008. *What is Balanced Literacy?* Saskatoon Public Schools http://olc.spsd.sk.ca/DE/PD/instr/strats/balancedliteracy/index.html.

Kohlberg, L. 1981. *The Philosophy of Moral Development*. New York: Harper and Row.

Kupper-Herr, B. 2000. "Conferencing with students about their writing." Retrieved 1/8/09 from http://emedia.leeward.hawaii.edu/writing/Conferencing.htm.

Lambros, A. 2002. *Problem-based Learning in K-8 Classrooms: A Teacher's Guide to Implementation*. Thousand Oaks, CA: Corwin Press.

Learning a-z.com. 2009. Reading a-z.com: Running record. Retrieved Jan. 23, 2009 from www.readinga-z.com/guided/runrecord.html.

Levine, M. 2002. *All Kinds of Minds*. New York: Simon and Schuster.

National Association for the Education of Young Children 1998. In *Young Children*, July 1998, 53 (4): 30–46. Retrieved 1/7/09 from http://74.125.47.132/search?q=cache:DJzJmO0fRBMJ:www.naeyc.org/about/positions/pdf/PSREAD98.PDF+developmentally+appropriate+readings&hl=en&ct=clnk&cd=1&gl=us.

National Center for Learning Disabilities 1999–2008. Emergent Literacy: Early Reading and Writing Development. Retrieved 1/3/09 from www.ncld.org/content/view/999/527/.

National Writing Project. 2008. "Teaching Writing." Retrieved 1/9/09 from www.nwp.org/cs/public/print/resouce_topic/teaching_writing.

Neil, J. 2005 John Dewey, the Modern Father of Experiential Education. Wilderdom. com. Retrieved 1/2/09 from http://wilderdom.com/experiential/Experiential-Dewey.html.

Opitz, M.F. 1998. *Flexible Grouping in Reading.* New York: Scholastic Professional Book Division.

Ornstein, A.C. and Levine, D.U. 2008. *Foundations of Education.* Boston: Houghton Mifflin.

Piaget, J. 1955. The construction of reality in the child. Trans. Margaret Cook. London: Routledge.

Public Schools of North Carolina, State Board of Education, Department of Public Instruction. 2008. Introduction to Curricular Integration. www.ncpublicschools. org/curriculum/artsed/resources/handbook/music/46introduction.

Rief, S.F. and Heimburge, J.A. 2006. *How to reach and teach all children in the inclusive classroom: Practical strategies, lessons, and activities.* 2nd ed. San Francisco: Jossey-Bass.

Seaman, D. F., & Fellenz, R. A. 1989. *Effective strategies for teaching adults.* Columbus: Merrill Publishing Co.

Simons, J.A., Irwin, D.B., and Drinnien, B.A. 1987. "Maslow's Hierarchy of Needs." From *Psychology: The search for understanding* (West Publishing Company, New York). Retrieved 1/2/09 from http://honolulu.hawaii.edu/intranet/committees/FacDevCom/guidebk/teachtip/maslow.ht.

Tomilson, C.A. 2001. *How to differentiate instruction in mixed-ability classrooms.* Alexandria, VA: Association for Supervision and Curriculum Development.

Vygotsky, L.S. 1978. *Mind in society: The development of higher psychological processes.* Cambridge, MA: Harvard UP.

Wiggins, G., and McTighe, J. 1998. *Understanding by design.* Alexandria, VA: The Association for Supervision and Curriculum Development.

Williams, J. 2003. *Promoting independent learning in the primary classroom: Enriching the primary curriculum—child, teacher, context.* London: Open UP.

Woolfolk, A. 2003. *Educational psychology.* Upper Saddle River, NJ: Pearson. www.nifl.gov/partnershipforreading/publications/PRFbooklet.pdf.

Mathematics

This chapter will provide you with information to help you identify the nature of mathematics instruction and the theories that help us understand how children in grades K-6 learn math. Similar to other chapters, this chapter will be divided into three areas: curriculum, instruction, and assessment. Before we get into these areas, we will begin with an examination of the standards introduced by the National Council of Teachers of Mathematics (NCTM). This list of standards helps teachers increase math literacy among students. Indeed, most math teachers address these standards within their instructional goals.

At all levels of elementary school, math instruction transcends computing and problem-solving. In 2000, the NCTM published standards for K-8 that detail what students should know and be able to do in terms of **content** and **process**.

These standards are ultimately connected to the school's curriculum and become the teacher's responsibility.

Curriculum Focal Points:

1. **Numbers sense**—Hamm and Adams (2008) explain that **number sense** is the idea that understanding numbers comes in stages. Students develop their number sense in five stages:

   Stage 1 No knowledge of numbers
   Stage 2 Understanding words like *a lot* or *seven* but can't compute
   Stage 3 Counting with errors

Stage 4 Counting with objects or on fingers

Stage 5 Solving problems

A teacher can teach number sense by devising counting games where students match numbers to objects.

2. **Geometry**—Students learn about shapes, first through concrete materials; then through a development of their vocabulary (shape, symmetry, congruity, etc.); and finally in middle school through more formal problem-solving.

3. **Measurement**—Students are asked to compare what is being measured (for example, circumference) with whatever unit is being used to measure (inches, centimeters, etc.). Students can interact concretely to learn this.

4. **Data analysis**— This stage encourages students to collect, organize, and relay information, often in a graph or chart. For instance, students might predict how often a die will land on 6, and then they make a chart of their findings.

5. **Numbers and operations**—This stage includes problem solving, wherein students respond to specific math problems. The teacher can help with this by having students draw a picture of the problem, use an equation, figure it out in his or her head, make a chart, etc. Students also create their own problems. Solving problems involves the use of reasoning—in this case, math helps students understand and explain their thinking processes. This is taught informally in the early elementary years when children are simply encouraged to explain terms like *all, none,* and *some.* In the older grades, reasoning involves inductive (examples lead to a general rule) vs. deductive reasoning (premises lead to a conclusion).

6. **Algebra**

    a. Patterns—One car has four tires, two cars have eight tires. How many tires do three cars have?

    b. Algebra—When variables are used and solved for $(2 + x = 5)$; finding the value of a variable in an equation.

The following table summarizes the curricular focal points from K-6 as they are outlined by the NCTM (2009). It is a meaningful overall guide to what content should be taught at level of elementary school.

Table 3.1 Scope and Sequence of Skills

Grade Level	Numbers, Orders, Values	Addition, Subtraction	Ratios, Measurements, Decimals	Fractions, Comparisons	Equations, Colors, Geometry	Multiplication, Division	Graph, Estimation, Solving
K	Count by 1s and 10s to 100 Count by 2s and 5s Write numbers to 10 Write families to 100 Use values of 10s and 1s place	Add single digits with no regrouping	Use penny, nickel, dime, dollar Tell time on half hour and hour Name days of week and seasons Identify cup and quart Read inches	Recognize $\frac{1}{2}, \frac{1}{3}, \frac{1}{4}$ Compare longer, shorter, taller, etc.	Recognize primary and secondary colors and black Recognize square, circle, and triangle Use *up, down, top* and *next*		Identify what comes next Read pictographs and simple bar graphs
1	Count by 1s, 2s, 5s, and 10s Use place values of 1s, 10s, and 100s place	Write and give addition facts from 1 to 18 Add with regrouping in the 1s place Subtract without regrouping	Name months and days Tell time on quarter hour Use nickel, dime, and quarter Identify pint and pound	Recognize $\frac{1}{2}, \frac{1}{3}$, $\frac{1}{4}, \frac{1}{5}, \frac{1}{6}, \frac{1}{8}$	Recognize circle, square, oval, diamond, triangle, and cube		Read bar graphs Identify height and length Round numbers using a number line
2	Identify even and odd numbers Use tally marks Use and explain the value of the 1,000s place	Add with carrying in 1s,10s, and 100s place Perform horizontal addition Solve word problems	Name months and their abbreviations Tell time on 5 minutes Perform money operations including $5, $10 and $20 bills Read a Fahrenheit thermometer Identify liquid and dry measures	Compare two numbers Read fraction words Identify fractional parts of groups and sets	Determine area, perimeter, and volume Recognize pyramid, pentagon, and hexagon	Use multiplication facts from 0 to 10	Round numbers, height, and time Read grids and line graphs

(continued)

Table 3.1 Scope and Sequence of Skills *(continued)*

Grade Level	Numbers, Orders, Values	Addition, Subtraction	Ratios, Measurements, Decimals	Fractions, Comparisons	Equations, Colors, Geometry	Multiplication, Division	Graph, Estimation, Solving
3	Read word numbers to 1 million Show expanded numbers Explain the properties of 1 and 0 Use the terms *add, tallymarks, greater than*	Use sum, estimating, borrowing, word problems Demonstrate carrying or regrouping in the 1s, 10s, and 100s place Use horizontal addition Solve word problems	Use Fahrenheit and Celsius measurements Use tenths Add and subtract dollars and cents Be able to use months and their abbreviations Tell time to 5 minutes Perform money operations Recognize $5, $10, and $20 bills Use both liquid and dry measures	Identify fractional parts of whole and sets Rename fractions Compare numbers using *greater than, less than, and equal* Use fraction words Demonstrate the use of fractional parts of groups Use sets to illustrate fractions and illustrate fractions with sets	Compute the volume of a cube Recognize rays, angles, congruent shapes, and prisms Compute area and perimeter of volume, pyramid, pentagon and hexagon	Use division facts from 1 to 10 Calculate 1- and 2- digit quotients with and without remainders Use multiplication facts from 0 to 10	Continue work with graphs and grids Round numbers to the 10,000 place Tell time accurately to the minute
4	Use values to 100 billion Use and recognize prime and composite Determine factors Give ordinal and cardinal numbers	Give addition properties Add and subtract numbers up to 6 digits Subtract with regrouping Subtract money	Use the terms am and pm Explain the term century Compute time in various time zones Use the prefixes *milli-, centi-, deci-, deca-, hecto-, kilo-* Convert fractions to decimals Perform operations on decimals and ratios Use equal ratios	Recognize fractional parts of whole and name them correctly Give word fractions Provide equivalent fractions Add and subtract fractions with like and unlike denominators	Recognize shapes and solids Use the terms *obtuse, vertex, ray, diameter, radius* Perform operations on equations	Calculate averages Use zeros in the quotient correctly Multiply 2- and 3- digit numbers	Compare and coordinate graphs

Table 3.1 Scope and Sequence of Skills *(continued)*

Grade Level	Numbers, Orders, Values	Addition, Subtraction	Ratios, Measurements, Decimals	Fractions, Comparisons	Equations, Colors, Geometry	Multiplication, Division	Graph, Estimation, Solving
5	Determine prime factors Use factor trees Use exponents Equal, not equal	Apply addition properties and facts Apply addition operation with 2 to 6 digits Determine missing addends Work with equations Subtract Estimate	Use standard and metric measure Count change Solve problems with ratios and percentages Figure amount of sales tax Determine discounts	Find least common multiples Solve problems with unlike denominators Perform operations on mixed numerals Rename numbers Reduce fractions to lowest terms	Use a compass and protractor Solve surface area problems Perform operations on fractions Recognize and use chords Classify polygons	Calculate mean, mode, and median Problem solve by choosing the proper operation Figure probability with one-variable problems Demonstrate ability to apply calculator math	Multiply 3-digit numbers Calculate averages with remainders Divide money Estimate quotients Determine division and multiplication properties
6	Round to 10s, 100s, 1,000s Use scientific notation Use the correct order of operations Use integers Calculate square roots	Continue addition and subtraction Continue to work with equations	Cross products Divide and multiply by 10, 100, 1,000 Determine equal ratios Use cross products to solve for *n*	Determine reciprocals Divide by fractions Perform operations on fractions Divide by whole and mixed numbers	Construct a right and equilateral triangle, a parallelogram, and a square Bisect an angle	Choose the proper operation Find patterns Set up budgets Apply some business math, such as figuring interest and balancing a checkbook	Divide using 4-digit divisors Estimate quotients Supply missing factors

CURRICULUM

Clearly, it is important for teachers to understand the aforementioned general expectations for each grade level. Moreover, there are certain areas of mathematical content and processes that students should learn. The following section will summarize this in the hopes that you will be able to analyze and apply the information on the 0012 exam.

First, it is crucial that students understand **number systems**. A **number** is an abstract idea used in mathematics for both counting and measuring. A symbol which represents a number is called a **numeral**, but in common usage the word number is used for both the abstract idea and the symbol. A number system is a set of numbers, such as natural numbers, integers, rational numbers, etc. **Natural numbers** are the familiar counting numbers (1,2,3...). **Negative numbers** are the opposite of a counting number (−1,−2,−3...). By opposite, we mean that if a natural number indicates positive, or credit, then a negative numbers indicate a debit. **Zero** identifies a null count. **Whole numbers** are the natural (counting) numbers and 0 (0,1,2,3...). **Integers** include the natural numbers, their negatives, and 0 (...−3,−2,−1,0,1,2,3...). **Even** describes a number that is divisible by 2 without a remainder, while **odd** indicates a number not divisible by 2.

A **multiple** is an integer which is multiplied by any other number. For instance, the multiples of 7 are 7, 14, and 21. On the other hand, a **divisor** is an integer which evenly divides n without leaving a remainder. For example, the positive divisors of 42 are 1, 2, 3, 6, 7, 14, 21, and 42. A divisor is also called a factor of n. A multiple of an integer is the product of that integer with another integer. In other words, a is a multiple of b if $a = nb$, where n is an integer.

PRAXIS Pointer

Write neatly. If the scorers can't read your responses, they can't score it accurately.

A **prime number** is an integer greater than 1 which is only divisible by 1 and itself. Examples of prime numbers include 2, 3, 5, 7, 11, and 13. However, a **composite number** is a positive integer which has a positive divisor other than one or itself. For instance, 14 is a positive integer that has 7 and 2 as divisors. Composite numbers include 4, 6, 8, 9, 10, and 12.

When it comes to **base-10 counting**, one can see that our numerical system is based on the power of 10. Base-10 counting happens when we write a larger number, meaning a number consisting of more than one digit. The order in which we write the number from left to right is significant. For instance, 123 has a different value than 321 and 213. This is because we give each place a value. The rightmost number is valued as written, the value of the next rightmost number is multiplied by 10, the next rightmost number is multiplied by 10 × 10, and so on.

This brings us to **expanded notation**, which shows the value of each number in its place. So 123 may thus be written as $(1 \times [10 \times 10]) + (2 \times [10 \times 1]) + (3 \times 1)$. Or we can write in **exponential notation**, in which 123 can be expressed as $(1 \times 10^2) + (2 \times 10^1) + (3 \times 10^0)$.

Operations

It is very important for students to understand the four main arithmetic **operations** since almost all of their future math instruction will be built on these operations.

Addition means to add, join, unite, or combine numbers into a **sum**. Addition is **commutative**, meaning that order does not matter $(1 + 2 = 2 + 1)$. It is also **associative**, meaning that the order of the grouping doesn't matter. For instance, $(2 + 3) + 1 = 2 + (3 + 1)$. It's important to note that while students may not know how to multiply, they can easily double numbers: 1 doubles to 2, 2 doubles to 4, etc. Early elementary teachers should point out to students that they are adding when they do this.

Subtraction means to remove or take away a number; the result is called a **difference.** Addition and subtraction are **inverses**; that is, they can cancel each other out. Thus, if we first add 10 and then subtract 10, we arrive at the same number where we started.

Multiplication may be thought of as repeated addition; for example, 4 multiplied by 3, often said as "4 times 3," can be represented as either 4 "3 times" or $4 + 4 + 4 = 12$. The result in multiplication is the **product.** Like addition, multiplication is **commutative**. If students are having trouble understanding multiplication, show them **the area rectangle**, which may be read as 4 nine times or 9 four times.

Figure 3.1 Area Rectangle

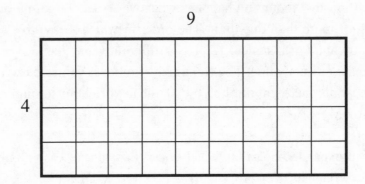

Division is the inverse of multiplication. The result is the **quotient**. So if, $c \times b = a$ then $\frac{a}{b} = c$. A special rule to keep in mind with respect to this equation is that a cannot be zero.

Regrouping is also known as *carrying*. Since when we add, the sums often result in values greater than 9, the value of ten is regrouped to the next column.

$$\begin{array}{r} 44 \\ + 22 \\ \hline 66 \end{array} \quad \text{no regrouping needed}$$

But what about this equation?

$$\begin{array}{r} 44 \\ + 88 \\ \hline 1212 \end{array}$$

Clearly that is not correct, because of our base-10 numerical system. We have to "carry" the 10, or regroup it.

$$\begin{array}{r} 5 \\ \cancel{44} \\ + 88 \\ \hline 132 \end{array}$$

The **order of operations** is another way to say: In a problem with different operations (addition, multiplication, etc.), which comes first? For example, $[(6/2) + 1 \times 3 - 1]$. To remember the order of operations, use the mnemonic: *Please Excuse My Dear Aunt Sally*, where P = parentheses, E = exponents, M = multiplication, D = division, A = addition, and S = subtraction. In our example we'd deal with the parentheses first: 6 divided by 2 is 3. Next is the multiplication: $1 \times 3 = 3$. Next is the addition $3 + 3 = 6$. Finally, the subtraction $6 - 1 = 5$. Another example is $7 + 2 \times 5 = 17$. If you don't use the order of operations, you could arrive at the wrong answer. For instance, this equation does not equal 45, but students might reach the wrong answer if they were to approach the problem as: $(7 + 2) \times 5 = 45$. Therefore, it's very important for students to understand the order of operations.

Rational numbers are numbers that can be written as fractions or decimals. They may be integers or non-integers. Non-integers are usually expressed as fractions. A **decimal** is a fraction written in different notation. All decimals are also fractions. For example, the fraction $\frac{1}{4}$ would be written as the decimal 0.25. A **percentage** is ratio of parts per hundred. It can be written as a decimal or with a number and a percent sign. For instance, if you got $\frac{1}{2}$ of the problems on the quiz right, you got .50 or 50 percent right. A percent is expressed from a decimal by moving the decimal point two places to the right and then adding a %.

In terms of **modeling the operations**, it is extremely important for students to understand the four main operations intuitively. Some exercises and models which have been successful are included. Initially, a good activity to use with students is to give them **concrete examples**, such as apples or poker chips. Once they understand the concrete models, the teacher can move on, perhaps using pictures of the objects on a worksheet, working with a **semi-concrete model**. Next, the teacher can add tally marks or x's, which is a **semi-abstract model**. At that point, the students are ready to understand the **abstract model**: $3 + 2 = 5$.

An easy way to make abstract concepts meaningful is through **number stories**. For example, the teacher can have each student write a simple equation $(5 - 3 = 2)$. Then, he or she can ask each student to think of a number story, such as *Mom made 5 cookies, and she gave Tom 3. That leaves two for me.*

Problem-solving

When it comes to **problem-solving**, many students find word problems the hardest part of math. By translating the word problem into a mathematical operation, solutions can be found easily. There are several key words in word problems that connote the proper operation to use. The following chart explains what words or phrases indicate which of the four main operations to use:

Addition — *added to, combined, increased by, more than, sum, together, total of, plus*
Subtraction — *decreased by, difference between, difference of, fewer than, less than, minus*
Multiplication — *increased by a factor of, multiplied by, product of, times*
Division — *decreased by a factor of, divide, equal groups, how many groups, how many to each, quotient, separate, share*

Another helpful strategy used in problem-solving is **estimation**. When students estimate, they make a rough calculation. Students often do this by **rounding**. For example, in the equation $99 + 11 = ?$, students might round 99 up to 100 and 11 down to 10, so $99 + 11$ is approximately 110. Other strategies students use when solving problems include making a table, chart, or list

or working backwards from answers to questions.

Algebraic Rules

- The operation of addition (+) . . .
  - is written $a + b$;
  - is **commutative**: $a + b = b + a$;
  - is **associative**: $(a + b) + c = a + (b + c)$;
  - has an **inverse operation** called subtraction: $(a + b) - b = a$, which is the same as adding a negative number, $a - b = a + (-b)$;
  - has a **special element** 0 which preserves numbers: $a + 0 = a$.

- The operation of **multiplication** ($\times$) . . .
  - is written $a \times b$ or $a \cdot b$;
  - is commutative: $a \times b = b \times a$;
  - is associative: $(a \times b) \times c = a \times (b \times c)$;
  - is abbreviated by juxtaposition: $a \times b \equiv ab$;
  - has a special element 1 which preserves numbers: $a \times 1 = a$;
  - has, for non-zero numbers, an inverse operation called division: $(ab)/b = a$, which is the same as multiplying by a **reciprocal**, $a/b = a(1/b)$;
  - **distributes** over addition: $(a + b)c = ac + bc$;

- The operation of **exponentiation** . . .
  - is written a^b;
  - means repeated multiplication: $a^n = a \times a \times \ldots \times a$ (n times);
  - is neither commutative nor associative: in general $a^b \neq b^a$ and $(a^b)^c \neq a^{(bc)}$;

Geometry

A **right triangle** has one 90° internal angle, known as a **right angle**. The side opposite to the right angle is the *hypotenuse*; it is the longest side in the right triangle. The other two (shorter) sides are the *legs* of the triangle.

Figure 3.2 Right Angle

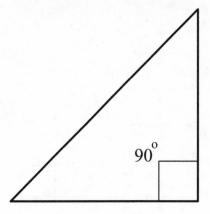

An **isosceles** triangle has two sides of equal length. An isosceles triangle also has two equal internal angles.

Figure 3.3 Isosceles Triangle

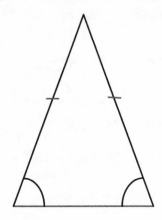

The **Pythagorean theorem** dictates that in any right triangle with legs a and b and a hypotenuse of c, the sum of the squares of the legs is equal to the square of the hypotenuse. This is expressed as $a^2 + b^2 = c^2$. In a triangle with sides 3, 4, and 5, $3^2 + 4^2 = 5^2$ or $9 + 16 = 25$.

It is also important for students to understand the **Cartesian coordinate system**. The Cartesian coordinate system, or rectangular coordinate system, can be used to describe geometric shapes as algebraic formulas. Each point can be uniquely represented by two numbers: the x-coordinate, or abscissa, and the y-coordinate, or the ordinate. For example, if a point lies 2 units on the x-axis and 3 units on the y-axis, then this point may be represented as point (2, 3). There are also negative numbers on the x and y axes.

Figure 3.4 Cartesian Coordinate System

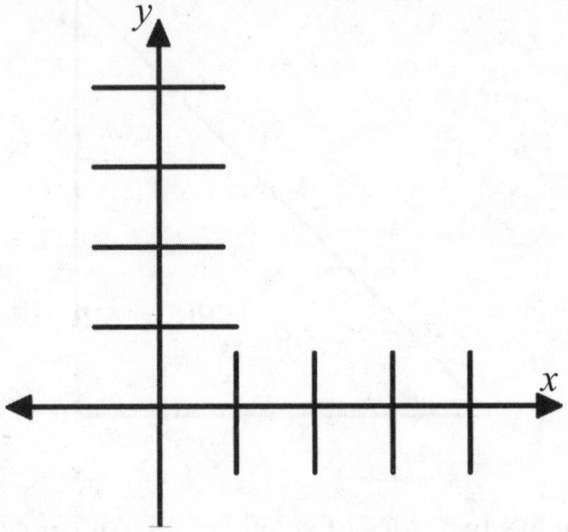

MEASUREMENT

Area: The area of a rectangle (including a square): length × width

> Area of a triangle : ½ × base × height
> Area of a circle: πr^2
> Area of a square: $s^2 = s \times s$ (where s is the length of a side)
> All squares are rectangles, but *not* all rectangles are squares.

Volume:

> A **cube**: $s^3 = s \times s \times s$ (where s is the length of a side)
> A **rectangular prism**: l × w × h (length, width, and height)
> A **cylinder**: $r^2 h$ (r = radius of circular face, h = distance between faces)
> A **sphere**: $\frac{4}{3} \pi r^3$ (r = radius of sphere)

Metric System: In the U.S., the customary units of measurement include inches, feet, and miles. The rest of the world uses the **metric system**. Mathematical manipulations which use the metric system are easier to calculate, because they are based on the base-10 number system.

> **kilo** = 1,000
> **centi** = 0.01
> **milli** = 0.001

meter (m) = SI unit of length (SI means "International System of Units")
second (s) = SI unit of time
kilogram (kg) = SI unit of mass

Measuring Temperature

We can measure temperature in **degrees Fahrenheit** (°F) or **degrees Celsius** (°C). The Celsius scale ranges between the freezing point (0°C) and boiling point (100°C) of pure water at sea-level. We can use two formulas for conversion:

degrees Fahrenheit $= C \times \frac{9}{5} + 32$

degrees Celsius $= (F - 32) \times \frac{5}{9}$

Measuring Angles

An angle is the figure formed by two rays which share a common endpoint.

acute = less than 90°
obtuse = greater than 90°
right = 90°

Time

Time is measured in seconds, minutes, hours, days, weeks, months, and years. A day is divided into 24 hours, a year is divided into 12 months or 52 weeks, and a minute is divided into 60 seconds. Time is measured in two standard blocks: a.m. and p.m., which come from the Latin "ante meridiem" (before noon) and "post meridiem" (after noon). There are time zones on the world map; one important divider is the International date line, which is in the Pacific ocean near Australia. When one crosses over it to the east, he or she starts that day over again; if one crosses it to the west, he or she skips ahead to the next day. In the U.S., time is divided into Eastern, Central, Mountain, and Pacific regions.

Statistics

Statistics is a branch of mathematics in which numbers are collected and compared in charts and graphs. The following concepts are important to know when it comes to statistics:

The **mean** is found by adding all the numbers in a set of data and then dividing the sum by the number of values.

The **mode** is the value that is most often repeated. Often, one refers to the mode in non-numerical situations. For instance, *the mode of all the first names in the school is John*. The mode may or may not be unique.

The **median** is the value separating the higher half from the lower half whereby you sort all values in ascending order and find the "middle" value.

1, 3, **12**, 15, 21

Take note that when working with an even number of numbers, the median is the *mean* of the two middle numbers. In the set of numbers

1, 7, 12, 14, 18, 24, the mean is 13.

The **range** is the difference between the largest and smallest numbers. In the set of numbers 1, 3, 5, 6, 12, the range is 11, because the difference between 12 and 1 is 11.

PROBABILITY

Probability simply means the likelihood or chance that something will happen. In math, probability is expressed as the number of desired outcomes divided by the number of all possible outcomes. If I desire heads and the outcomes are heads and tails, the probability is

heads (1)—the desired outcome
(heads + tails) 2—all possible outcomes
$\frac{1}{2} = 50\%$
The probability of a coin flip is 50%.

The probability of a die landing on a one is 1/6, because the die has six faces, only one of which has a 1.

It is important for teachers to make sure students understand that every event is *independent* in this case. The probability of flipping heads is 50%. But what if I flip 10 tails in a row? The probability of flipping heads on the next toss is still 50% of flipping heads. The probability is **constant** and **does not change**.

TEACHING MATHEMATICS

Generally speaking, math teachers should create learning environments that transcend procedures and facts. They should encourage inquiry with each question and problem presented. Furthermore, they should help students build from their prior conceptual knowledge. Another very important area in math instruction is **communication**. This is inevitable in the mathematics class itself, as students have to communicate with each other when they are solving problems together. Teachers should give students the opportunity to do so.

Everyday Mathematics, a comprehensive pre-K−6 mathematics curriculum developed by the University of Chicago School Mathematics Project (2009), allows students to make connections between math and their everyday lives through direct teacher instruction, self-direction in the classroom, and reinforcement at home. Furthermore, **manipulatives** (blocks or other small pieces) help children to conceptualize when it comes to addition, subtraction, multiplication, and division.

It is very important to include hands-on, concrete examples throughout class because it will help the abstract concepts to be more easily understood. Many activities using manipulatives can be made into games. Following is a list of useful materials:

- For pre-numerical students, poker chips make excellent counting devices. They can even begin to add and takeaway some of the chips to learn addition and subtraction.
- An excellent manipulative is a set of base-10 blocks. These blocks allow students to "see" and "feel" regrouping and base-10. They can be used solo, in groups, or with a partner. One suggestion is to have a partner say a number and then having the student build that number.
- A set of number cards is also helpful. You can show associative properties of addition, place numbers, or say a three digit number and have each student show it represented with their number cards.
- An excellent tool is standard playing cards. Here is a game that is used in Everyday Mathematics:

  Addition Top It: Two to three students use a deck of playing cards, numbered 0–10. The cards are shuffled and the deck is placed in the middle of the players. Each player takes two cards and adds them together. The player with the highest sum wins that round and takes the other player's cards. The game is over when there are not enough cards left for each person to pull two cards. The person with the most cards at the end of the game wins.

Teachers should ask **leading questions** instead of giving the students the answers. They should also encourage students to draw pictures to help solve problems. Take the following example:

> On "School Spirit Day," students are required to wear school colors. In a classroom of 40 students, 20 are wearing green shirts, 5 are wearing blue pants, and 5 are not wearing either a green shirt or blue pants. How many are wearing both a green shirt and blue pants?

To solve this problem, it would help to draw a **Venn diagram** of the situation.

Figure 3.5 Venn Diagram: School

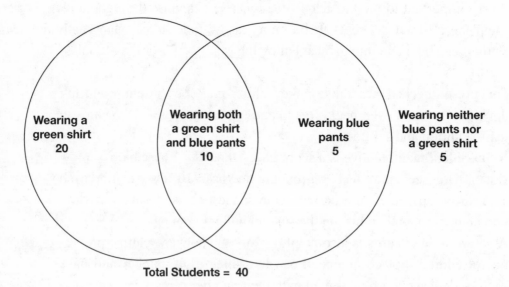

Similarly, teachers can reach out to visual learners by displaying information on the board using **flow charts, concept maps**, and **graphic organizers**. Students can "think aloud" about problems in pairs or small groups.

In general, teachers should use a **problem-based approach** to learning whereby they start a unit by giving the students a meaningful problem to solve (Posamentier, Hartman, & Kaiser 1998). They can ask students to **access their prior knowledge** about a concept before directly instructing the students about

PRAXIS Pointer

Practice explaining the key concepts covered in the review material.

it. They can show students **model problems** with solutions, explain how the concept applies to the real world, and incorporate **review** into their plans. In addition to putting students into groups for **cooperative learning** activities, they should work with individual students as often as possible. Teachers should encourage students to move from basic mathematics skills (such as reading the problem) to higher-level math skills, such as understanding, solving, checking the solution, and observing other students solving problems in different ways (Artzt & Armour-Thomas 1992).

As Posamentier, Hartman, and Kaiser (1998) point out, the "Thinking Mathematics Project" has basic principles that can be used in the classroom to improve learning. The model includes:

- Establishing a strong sense of numbers through counting and estimation
- Basing instruction on situational story problems
- Accepting and soliciting multiple solutions and perhaps even more than one correct answer
- Requiring students to explain and justify their thinking
- Using a variety of teaching strategies
- Using ongoing assessment to guide instruction

In general, **homework assignments** should be carefully selected, teachers should collaborate with parents, and teachers should foster positive attitudes among students toward mathematics by making the subject fun — using games, giving praise, acknowledging mistakes, etc.

It is also important to note that in 1991, the NCTM developed six professional standards for teachers of mathematics to follow. They are:

Standard 1: Worthwhile mathematical tasks: Tasks should be engaging, stimulating, and thoughtful.

Standard 2: Teacher's Role in Discourse: Teachers should question, clarify, figure out when to go in depth, and monitor student participation.

Standard 3: Students Role in Discourse: The math classroom should be a place where communication, investigation, and varied ways of solving problems are acknowledged.

Standard 4: Tools for Enhancing Discourse: A multiplicity of tools should be used in a mathematics classroom, including computers, calculators, pictures, tables, and graphs.

Standard 5: Learning Environment: The teacher should help students by encouraging them to work independently and with each other through individual, small group, and direct instruction.

Standard 6: Analysis of Teaching and Learning: This is an ongoing process to reflect upon the student learning that is taking place in a math class and to make changes to teaching plans accordingly.

An elementary education teacher can try to introduce a **calculator activity** with students. Here's an example:

> **Beat the Calculator**: Three students play in groups: one player is the "caller," a second player is the "calculator," and the third is the "brain." The caller begins by selecting two cards from a deck of playing cards (0–9), and created an equation using the two numbers on the cards. This is a fact problem. The calculator then solves the problem with a calculator as the brain solves it without a calculator. Students try to race each other to get the correct answer first. The caller decides who got the answer first and that person wins the round. The players trade roles every 3–5 minutes, depending on how much time is available.

Nothing has changed life more for the classroom teacher than the **computer**. It is very important to integrate technology seamlessly into the classroom.

Spreadsheet programs such as Microsoft Excel and Lotus 123 are excellent aids to demonstrate math techniques. These programs can sum functions, sort numbers, and allow students to make formulas, macros, etc. In addition, the programs are excellent at creating pre-formatted bar, line, and pie charts after entering data.

Many teachers like to use a presentation program such as Microsoft PowerPoint to help guide and visually engage their students during classroom instruction. Teachers can also use interactive CD-ROMs or other programs to let students practice equations.

Lastly, the Internet has countless websites which are geared toward teaching math in a fun and inviting way.

When it comes to instruction, it is very important to keep the classroom **motivated**. A teacher should try to mix lectures with manipulatives, games, hands-on activities, partner work, handouts, independent work, and reviews.

ASSESSMENT IN MATHEMATICS

The NCTM published *Assessment Standards for School Mathematics* in 1995. It includes the "Mathematics Assessment Standards" with six guidelines for designing a meaningful assessment program. Specifically, assessments should let students demonstrate:

Standard 1: Mathematics
Standard 2: Learning
Standard 3: Equity (everyone has had an opportunity to learn)
Standard 4: Openness (teacher, student, and others should have access to the design process of the assessment)
Standard 5: Inference (the assessment should promote valid inferences about mathematics learning)
Standard 6: Coherence (the assessment process should be unified and consistent)

Teachers can also use images when constructing assessments. Examples of this technique are almost limitless. For instance, the teacher can show the class an image of a sporting event and then ask each student to create a story problem using the image. Or the teacher can display an ad from the newspaper and ask students to find an item for sale and then calculate the cost after a 20% discount.

It is very important to accurately assess students not just formally but also informally through all of the stages of the learning process.

During group and individual work, the teacher should observe his or her students' level of knowledge, questions, and grasp of the material. The teacher should write down a checklist of skills and competencies expected at each stage.

Projects, essays, portfolios, and paper and pencil tests are examples of **formal evaluation methods**. To assess the level of the student's work, it is important to be clear and objective when giving and grading a test. A **grading rubric** can help with this.

REFERENCES

Arzt, A., and Armour-Thomas, E. 1992. Development of cognitive-metacognitive framework for protocol analysis of group problem solving in mathematics. *Cognition and Instruction,* 9(2), 137–175.

Hamm, M., and Adams, D. 2008. *Differentiated instruction for K-8 math and science: Ideas, activities, and lesson plans.* Larchmont, NY: Eye on Education.

Heddens, J.W. and Speer, W.R. 1995. *Today's mathematics: Part 2-Activities and instructional ideas.* 9th ed. Upper Saddle River, NJ: Merrill.

National Council of Teachers of Mathematics (NCTM). 1995. *Assessment Standards for Teaching Mathematic*s. Reston, VA: NCTM.

National Council of Teachers of Mathematics (NCTM). 2008. *Curriculum Focal Points.* Retrieved December 29, 2008 from http//www.nctm.org/focalpoints.

National Council of Teachers of Mathematics (NCTM). 1991. *Professional Standards for Teaching Mathematics.* Reston, VA: NCTM.

Posamentier, A.S., Hartman, H.J., and Kaiser, C. (1998). *Tips for the mathematics teacher: Research based strategies to help students learn.* Thousand Oaks, CA: Corwin.

The University of Chicago School Mathematics Project. 2009. Everyday mathematics. Retrieved 2/9/09 from http://everydaymath.uchicago.edu.

CHAPTER 4

Science and Social Studies

This chapter will provide a curricular and instructional overview of K-6 Science and Social Studies as it pertains to the 0012 exam. It also gives information about assessment options that these teachers have. We begin with the area of science.

SCIENCE CURRICULUM

Certain state and national standards define what elementary education students need to learn in science. Specifically, in its 2002 statement on elementary school science, the National Science Teacher's Association emphasized coordinating learning between grade levels so students can transition from grade to grade. The NSTA describes an inquiry approach to the learning, and insists that for this type of program to be successful, science teachers not only need to be able to communicate with each other, but time must also be allotted for planning and teacher training. The curriculum must encourage problem solving in the scientific and technological context of our larger world. NSTA (2002) explains that any elementary science program must give students the chance to cultivate their skills and overall understanding so they can become scientifically literate; that is to say, they can describe, ask questions, construct explanations, test them against current scientific knowledge, and explain their findings to others. NSTA (2002) asserts that primary grade students learn science when:

1. They are involved in first-hand exploration and investigation and inquiry/process skills are nurtured.
2. Instruction builds directly on the student's conceptual framework.
3. Content is organized on the basis of broad conceptual themes common to all science disciplines.
4. Mathematics and communication skills are an integral part of science instruction. (NSTA 2002)

NSTA (2002) promotes the use of a number of teaching modes by the instructor in an effort to reach different learning styles. Moreover, students should be encouraged to discuss, work in groups, and share their findings. A multicultural and interdisciplinary effort should be made in the sciences. Likewise, teacher preparation and professional development must give teachers the chance to build classrooms that are hands-on, appropriate in terms of content, and positive with respect to attitudes about science and technology. NSTA maintains that teachers should go to conferences and meetings. They must also be able to rely on school administrators and community members to promote elementary science through materials, resources, and outside events. In terms of assessment, NSTA (2002) says that teachers must ensure that assessments measure problem-solving—applying concepts, asking questions, and processing information. For instance, assessments must reflect the purpose for which the learning was intended. Teachers also need to keep themselves abreast of advances in science education.

In 1996, the National Academies Press published the National Science Education Standards (NSES), a list of eight categories of science content standards:

1. Unifying concepts and processes in science
2. Science as inquiry
3. Physical science
4. Life science
5. Earth and space science
6. Science and technology
7. Science in personal and social perspectives
8. History and nature of science

In addition to these general standards, NSES (1996) provided a number of lists of "Less Emphasis/More Emphasis" conditions for teaching standards, professional development standards, assessment standards, science content standards, and science education system (federal, state, and district) standards.

NSES (1996) explained that it is important to de-emphasize traditional, lecture-based methods and to stop treating all students as if they are the same. Instead, science teachers should differentiate instruction, guide students through the inquiry process, and collaborate with other teachers. They should utilize a variety of methods to facilitate the class. Assessments should be conducted in an effort to gauge and build on what students understand. The move is away from merely knowing facts and instead toward understanding and integrating concepts, analyzing and synthesizing information, and forming and defending conclusions.

When it comes to planning science units, it is important to sequence the units and to build on prior knowledge the students have gained from other units and classes. For example, before the class studies chemical reactions, the teacher should ensure that the students have a firm grasp of the periodic table of the elements, the structure of the atom, and the makeup of subatomic particles. Very often, units are planned around themes. For instance, as Lemlech (1994) discusses, a theme such as "patterns of change" might include a discovery science activity that challenges first grade students to make a rainbow by giving them water-filled jars and taking them outside on a sunny day.

SCIENCE INSTRUCTION

Methods

The **scientific method** is not a specific set of steps that are meticulously followed, but rather a process of observation and analysis designed to develop a reliable, consistent, and objective representation and understanding of our world. The processes that make up the scientific method include identifying a problem or question; observing/ investigating/describing; recording data, formulating hypotheses; making predictions based on the hypotheses; testing hypotheses; interpreting results; and drawing conclusions.

Control variables are the **independent variables** for which the investigator knows the outcome, whereas **experimental variables** are **dependent variables** for which no one knows the outcome. For instance, if a new cancer drug is going through a drug trial, the pharmaceutical company will do a double-blind study in which some participants will get the control variable (the placebo) while others will get the experimental variable (the drug that is in its trial run).

When it comes to **scientific experimentation**, the following terms are important:

Observation: The act of sensing some measurable phenomenon.

Organization: Relating parts to a coherent whole.

Experimentation: Testing the effect of an independent variable on a dependent variable in a controlled environment.

Inference: Reaching a conclusion from a measurement or observation that is not explicit. For instance, one can infer that a class of 10 students has 6 girls if one knows it has 4 boys.

Prediction: Stating the outcome of an experiment in advance of doing it.

Scientists use certain **measuring instruments** such as microscopes, telescopes, spectroscopes, Petri dishes, test tubes, computers, etc. These instruments help scientists quantify data.

In an experiment, the scientist tests a **hypothesis**, or educated guess. The scientist or student identifies the relevant variables, identifies equipment and apparatus to be used to measure and record the variables, eliminates or suppresses other factors that could manipulate measured variables, and decides on a means of analyzing the data obtained. Ethically, the scientist is bound to either validate or disprove the hypothesis.

Findings, or **data**, must be collected and communicated either orally or in writing through graphs, diagrams, maps, models or charts. Sometimes, results are averaged or otherwise computed using **mathematics**. When a graph is used to plot raw data, the control variable is usually displayed on the *x*-axis of a graph (the horizontal line), while the experimental/dependent variable is usually displayed on the *y*-axis (vertically).

As the NSTA (2002) asserted, an inquiry approach to learning in science is used by the most effective science teachers. To engage in inquiry, a student must be able to acquire information from a variety of resources and organize and interpret that information. Inquiry may involve designing and conducting investigations that lead to the identification of issues which are important to analyze. Since different questions lead to different hypotheses, they each require different approaches and tools in the investigation stage of the process. Inquiry is essential for examining single topics or integrated topics within the sciences. Effective methods to engage in inquiry include:

- Determining the type of scientific investigation (for example, experimentation, systematic observation) that best addresses a given question or hypothesis

- Demonstrating a knowledge of considerations and procedures, including safety practices, related to designing and conducting experiments
- Recognizing how to use methods, tools, technologies, and measurements to gather and organize data

Scientific inquiry is **inductive**, meaning students first ask questions and collect data before they make generalizations and draw conclusions. Therefore, an inquiry lesson might begin with a thought-provoking question posed by the teacher, after which he or she guides the students in brainstorming a list of what they already know about the topic and then categorizing the resulting items. Students use these categories for group or individual research. Finally, students present their findings to the class. As the teacher facilitates this process, students are required to take responsibility for their own learning.

In addition to scientific inquiry, **accident** is a process that can lead to new scientific ideas or discoveries. For instance, gravity was famously discovered when Sir Isaac Newton happened to observe an apple falling from a tree.

It is important to note that **ethics** relate to scientific inquiry. For instance, it is unethical to do tests on people that will harm them. Likewise, it is important to point out to students that throughout history, many scientific explanations have been difficult for people to recognize because they were so different from what people previously believed. Indeed, science has the powerful potential to change accepted ways of thinking. One needs only to reflect on Galileo's notion that the earth revolves around the sun to realize how major a discovery that was and how it changed humankind's whole sense of center. Similarly, Darwin's theory of evolution directly challenged the notions of creation. In addition to helping students understand the impact of science, it is essential to help them realize that in the larger world, hundreds of scientists are using scientific inquiry to pursue complex undertakings such as finding the cures for cancer, AIDS, and a whole host of other diseases.

The following lesson on pollution, from Discovery Education (2009), utilizes scientific inquiry. The **objective** for the lesson is that students will see how pollution affects their immediate environment. The **materials** include latex gloves, collection bags, poster board, and markers. In terms of the actual **lesson**, the teacher begins by asking students, "What is pollution? What kinds of human processes create it?" After students give examples of pollution, the teacher has the students put on gloves and gather up some collection bags. The teacher brings the class to an outside area where there is litter. In small groups, the students collect the garbage. Back inside of the class, they talk about the types of garbage they found and how the pollution could have been avoided in the first place. Then, the students create posters that encourage recycling. Clearly, this lesson demonstrates scientific inquiry in that it begins with questions that students answer through reflection and formulation of conclusions based on their experiences.

Math and technology definitely assist students in different kinds of scientific inquiry; indeed, the three areas greatly overlap. Therefore, as Adams and Hamm (1998) point out, the three approaches can be integrated in the classroom in cooperative learning activities.

SCIENCE CONTENT

Earth Science

The Structure of the Earth

The major **layers** of the earth are the **crust, mantle, outer,** and **inner core**. The inside of the earth is hot, with lots of pressure. **Plates** are large, moving sections of the earth, created by faults, earthquakes, volcanoes, and mountains. There are three types of rocks: **igneous** (formed from molten rock), **sedimentary** (formed from the deposit of sediments) and **metamorphic** (formed from the application of heat and pressure to both sedimentary and metamorphic rocks).

Soil is formed from the breakdown of rocks through weathering by wind, water, heat, and rain. **Minerals** are natural, non-living particles that are the building blocks of rock. They give rocks their color, hardness, texture, density, and luster. **Fossils** are the buried remains of plants and animals that have existed in rocks for thousands of years.

About 75 percent of the earth is covered with water, which is called the **hydrosphere** (oceans). The **four oceans** are the Atlantic, Pacific, Indian, and Arctic, and they are composed of salt water. There are certain physical features at the shore and beneath the oceans. The shore has sand dunes and beaches, while what is beneath the ocean is made up of ridges, valleys, plains, and mountain ranges. The various **gases that make up the atmosphere** are, in descending order: nitrogen, oxygen, carbon dioxide, and trace gases. The atmosphere has several layers: the **thermosphere, mesosphere,**

> **PRAXIS Pointer**
>
> By becoming familiar with the structure of the test, you can save time when you begin taking the actual test. In addition, you can cut your chances of experiencing any unwanted surprises.

stratosphere, and **troposphere**. The **Aurora Borealis** is caused by electrons, or charged particles, interacting with the atmosphere. It is displayed in the layer of the atmosphere called the **ionosphere**, a small part or extension of the thermosphere which is not considered a layer on its own. **Air pressure** is the weight of the air pressing down on the earth's surface, measured by pounds per square inch.

Processes of the Earth

As was previously stated, **weathering** is the process of breaking down rocks and soil through wind, water, rain, heat, ice, and snow. **Erosion** is the wearing away of the surface of the earth through water, rain, wind, and ice.

A **volcano** is an opening, or rupture, in the earth's surface which allows magma, or molten rock from beneath the earth's crust, to escape from deep below the surface. A zone of frequent earthquakes and volcanic eruptions which encircle the basin of the Pacific Ocean in the shape of a horseshoe is known as the **Ring of Fire**. An **earthquake**, or a trembling or shaking movement of the Earth's surface, occurs as a result of **plate tectonics**. When the earth's plates are moving against each other, a build-up of stress can cause an earthquake.

Currents are movements of the surface of the ocean caused by blowing wind or moving ice. **Waves** are swells and depressions of water moving on the surface of oceans. **Tides** are the regular rise and fall of waters in the oceans and seas that are caused by the pull of the moon's gravity on the earth.

The **water cycle** is made up of evaporation, condensation, and precipitation. **Clouds** are made up of water, vapor, and ice. There are different types of clouds: *cirrus, cirrostratus, cirrocumulus, altostratus, altocumulus, stratocumulus, stratus, cumulus,* and *cumulonimbus*. There are also different types of precipitation: rain, snow, hail, ice, sleet, dew, drizzle, fog, and freezing rain. There are also different types of precipitation: rain, snow, hail, ice, sleet, dew, drizzle, fog, and freezing rain. In terms of measuring pressure and temperature on a map, an **isobar** is a line on a map connecting equal points of pressure, while an **isotherm** is a line on a map connecting equal points of temperature.

Earth History

The universe is defined as everything that physically exists: the entirety of space and time, all forms of matter, energy, and momentum. The present universe is believed to have begun at the time of the "**big bang**," about 13.7 billion years ago. Scientists speculate that all matter in the universe was concentrated into an infinitely hot dense ball until a huge explosion sent all mass and matter expanding across the universe. The matter began to cool and form into planets and other heavenly bodies. The **origin of the earth** began when the earth formed approximately 4.6 billion years ago. We measure the time on earth on a geologic time scale because of the large span of time the earth has been around. The time since the formation of earth can be broken down into four eras. The **Cenozoic** (the present, began 65 million years ago with a mass extinction), **Mesozoic** (the age of dinosaurs, 65–251 million years ago), **Paleozoic** (simple life forms become complex, 251–542 million years ago), and **Precambrian** (very simple life forms evolve such as bacteria and algae, before 542 million years ago). We can tell a lot about these time periods by examining rocks and dating them, which is known as the **rock record**. **Paleontologists** can also look at **fossils**, which are the remains of ancient animals in the rock record. For instance, in the layers of rock which formed prior to 65 million years ago, a large number of fossils have been found, but there have been very few fossils of any animals found from after that time. Scientists have deduced that a large number of animals perished at that time. In the rock record, scientists in Mexico also found evidence of a crater which formed around this time. This is why scientists believe that dinosaurs died from a meteoric impact.

The Earth in the Universe

Within the universe, there are a variety of heavenly bodies. A **star** is a bundle of light-emitting gas. A **comet** is a form of flying ice with a long tail, while a **meteor** is a flying rock that is orbiting in space. An **asteroid** is simply a large meteor. **Galaxies** are large groups of stars, an example being our galaxy, the **Milky Way**.

The **solar system** is made up of our sun and all the planets and other heavenly bodies that orbit it. The **planets** in our solar system move out from the sun as follows: Mercury, Venus, Earth, Mars, Jupiter, Saturn, Uranus, Neptune, and Pluto (which is no longer considered a planet due to its low mass). The inner planets are generally smaller, warmer, and made of rock; the outer planets are larger, colder, and made of gas. In a **solar eclipse**, the moon obstructs the view between the earth and the sun. In a **lunar eclipse**, the moon is hidden behind the earth's shadow. It is important to understand the relationship between the earth, moon, and sun: the earth orbits around the sun every 365 days. This orbit and the tilt of the earth's axis are what cause the seasons. When the Northern Hemisphere is tilted away from the sun, it experiences winter. This is also why when the U.S. has winter, Australia has summer; the Northern and Southern Hemisphere experience opposite seasons. Furthermore, the earth rotates every 24 hours; this rotation causes day and night.

Life Science

Living Systems: Their Structures and Functions

The smallest structural units of living organisms are called **cells**. Each cell has a **nucleus, cytoplasm,** and a **cell wall**. **Photosynthesis** takes place when light's energy is changed into food for plants. **Diffusion** is the flow of particles from areas of higher concentration to areas of lower concentration. For example, amino acids in cells may move from regions of high concentration to low. **Osmosis** is the process of diffusion of water through a semi-permeable membrane. **Active transport** requires energy to move molecules across a membrane, because the molecules are moving against a concentration gradient, from a low concentration to a higher one. **Transpiration** is the evaporation of water from plant leaves into the atmosphere. **Respiration** is how an organism burns sugar and releases carbon dioxide.

Humans have **circulatory systems**, responsible for internal transport in the body. Blood pumps in the heart, the veins bring it to the heart, and the arteries bring it away from the heart. Likewise, humans have **digestive systems** to receive and process food. This system includes the mouth, esophagus, stomach, small intestine, and large intestine.

Reproduction and Heredity

In **sexual reproduction**, the method of repopulation for humans and most other animals, there is a male and a female, and reproduction is marked by **meiosis** and **fertilization**. Conversely, in **asexual reproduction**, only one parent is involved, and the organism in effect reproduces on its own (for example, it splits in half or forms spores).

The **human life cycle** begins when the egg and sperm unite to form a **zygote** which develops into an **embryo**. When it has matured, generally after nine months of gestation, a child is born. Through the first year of life, a person is called an infant. The infant learns to walk and becomes a toddler and then proceeds into childhood. **Adolescence** is the next stage, from roughly age 12–18 years. In this stage, starting with puberty, boys become men and girls become women. During this time, the human is getting ready for adulthood, growing to his or her maximum size and becoming physically able to reproduce. **Adulthood** is the time when people learn to provide for themselves. The life cycle usually starts over again during this stage, when adults reproduce. The final stage of the life cycle is **old age**, when the body begins to break down.

A **gene** is a hereditary unit located on a chromosome which determines the characteristics of the organism. There are **dominant** and **recessive traits**. A dominant trait overrides a recessive trait. For instance, if both parents have brown eyes, their offspring can have blue eyes only if the recessive trait for blue eyes is passed down on both sides and the offspring do not receive a dominant brown-eyed gene from either parent.

The Life Cycle and Evolution

In terms of the behavior of living things, **migration** is when living things move from one region to another (for example, birds flying south). On the other hand, **hibernation** means going to sleep or becoming dormant for the winter. **Conditioned behavior** occurs when an animal is trained to respond to specific stimuli or circumstances. For instance, a dog may salivate when it hears a bell because it has been conditioned to know that means it will get a treat. **Adaptation** is how living things adjust. For instance, if the fruit is high in the tree, the animals with longer necks will preferentially survive through the process of **natural selection** in which some animals live and some die. This relates to Darwin's idea of **survival of the fittest:** basically, it is the notion that the strongest survive. **Extinction** occurs when the entire population of an organism dies out.

Interdependence of Living Things

Communities are groups of plants and animals living and interacting under the same conditions near each other. An **ecosystem** is an ecological community of plants and other organisms which co-exist in the same physical environment. Within the ecosystem, there is a **food chain** in which lower members on the chain are eaten by higher members. In **Figure 4.1**, larger and smaller fish eat bivalves (e.g., mollusks) which eat zooplankton, that in

Figure 4.1 Food Web

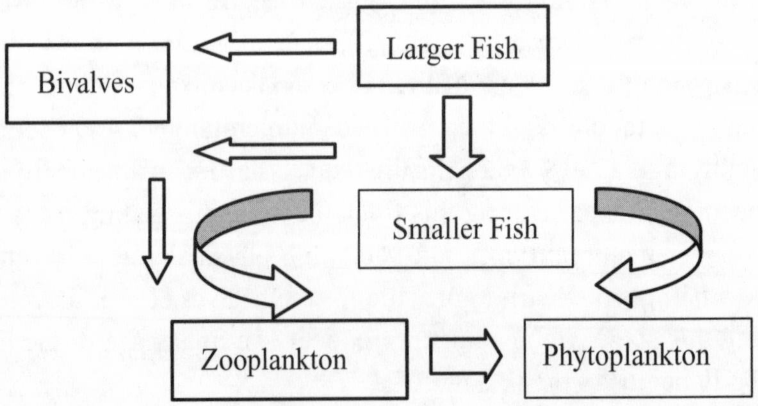

turn eat phytoplankton. If certain kinds of organisms are introduced or removed from the food chain, much of the food chain dies. A great example of this happened at the end of the Cretaceous period (about 65 million years ago) when a meteorite is believed to have hit the earth, kicking up huge amounts of dust. The dust blocked the sun, shutting off photosynthesis, and all of the plants and dinosaurs died. The **food web** explains how animals form interconnected food chains. Rarely can ecosystems be accurately represented by a food chain; it is a much more complex interaction better represented by a web.

Physical Science

Matter

Matter is anything that has mass and volume. Matter may take one of three **forms**: solid, liquid, or gas. **Physical changes** of matter do not involve a chemical composition change, whereas **chemical changes** change the composition of matter. An example of a physical change would be boiling water, since the molecules are still H_2O molecules, just in a different state. A good example of a chemical change would be iron rusting, since a new compound, iron oxide, forms. Students can recognize when a chemical reaction has taken place because energy is given off or absorbed, such as when you dissolve a substance or burn it. In a **mixture**, two things bind chemically, whereas in a **solution** two or more substances do not chemically bind. **Atoms** are the smallest invisible particles of an element. All **elements** are composed of atoms, and they are arranged in order of increasing atomic number on the **periodic table**. **Chemical equations** exist when one adds elements together into a **compound** ($C + O = CO$).

Forces and Motion

Motion is when something moves from one place to another. There is a relationship between speed, distance, and time: $D = R \times T$. **Acceleration** is velocity (or speed) squared. **Newton's laws of motion** express his theory of gravity: in essence, what goes up must also come down. Changes in **momentum** cause an object in motion to either accelerate or slow down. **Friction** is drag on an opposing force; another kind of force is **centripetal force**, which occurs when one goes around in a circle. **Mass** is the quantity of matter of an object, while **weight** is the strength of the gravitational pull on an object times its mass. If an object is in a state of **equilibrium**, all external and internal forces are balanced and the object is stable or unchanging. An object can have several forces acting on it and still be at rest. For instance, if I am standing still outside, I am still experiencing a variety of forces: the movement of the air, the gravity of the earth that is keeping me on the ground, and the rotation of the earth which I can't even detect.

Energy

It is important to understand the difference between **potential** (rock at the top of a mountain) versus **kinetic** (rock tumbling down the mountain) forms of energy. **Electric energy** can be converted into **heat energy** (an example being a space heater), into **light energy** (as evidenced by a light bulb), or into **motion** (as in an electric car). Since light travels faster than sound, we hear the sound of thunder before we see the flash of lightening that accompanies it. Speaking of sound, **echoes** are sound waves that bounce off of walls. The **electromagnetic spectrum** is made up of light waves, but there are also **non-visible waves** such as infrared waves, radios waves, microwaves, and x-rays.

Science in Personal and Social Perspectives

Personal Health

Nutrition (eating the right foods) and **physical fitness** (cardiovascular, muscle building, and stress-relieving exercises) help a person stay healthy. There are many **communicable diseases**, such as the flu and AIDS. **Infections** are spread when individuals are exposed to unfavorable conditions like unhygienic or contaminated environments. Drugs, alcohol, and tobacco are bad for the body because they impair brain function and that of other organs. Some diseases are **viral** (cold, flu, chicken pox) while others are **bacterial** (streptococcus, staphlococcus, and E. Coli). **Vaccinations** give individuals a low or weakened dose of the virus, enough so that the body doesn't get sick but instead develops antibodies against that virus.

Acid rain contains exhaust pollution from the environment. It's also important to know about **the greenhouse effect**: increases in CO_2 emissions trap heat in our environment and warm the oceans. In an effort to deal with air pollution, a community can reduce emissions by driving hybrid vehicles, carpooling, or using alternative forms of transportation like bicycles. To avoid water pollution, people can correctly dispose of hazardous household products and avoid dumping toxic waste.

Science, Technology, and Society

Clearly, science has direct links with technology, and teachers should emphasize that point. Historically, technology has provided scientists with instruments for inquiry, such as x-ray machines which can look at bones beneath the surface by measuring electromagnetic radiation. Technology will continue to enhance efforts at scientific inquiry.

ASSESSMENT IN TEACHING SCIENCE

Lemlech (1996) asserts that teachers of science should engage in several activities when assessing students. First, they should observe their performance in group work, experiments, discussions, and projects. Secondly, they should listen to how students communicate with each other about science. In addition, they should ask students to keep written reports in an effort to understand what they know. They should ask students to draw graphs to demonstrate their understanding of certain processes. They should work on projects which demonstrate their knowledge. After performing experiments, they should display their learning by answering written questions and writing essays. Furthermore, they should be evaluated for their knowledge of scientific concepts by using short answer and multiple-choice tests questions.

SOCIAL STUDIES AND ITS CURRICULUM

The term *social studies* describes the expansive study of various fields which involve past and current human behavior and interactions. Social studies teachers provide a broad and integrated overview of human behavior as it relates to history, geography, awareness of other cultures, political science, civics and society, sociology, psychology, anthropology, and economics. Generally, social studies teachers help students expand on their prior knowledge and develop higher order critical thinking skills so that they can ask the right questions and develop opinions about the world around them. The following section is divided into three categories that are important for the 0012 test: curriculum, instruction, and assessment.

In 2009, the National Council for the Social Studies (NCSS) outlined ten thematic curricular standards for social studies instruction. In essence, the NCSS maintains that social studies programs should include ten specific across elementary, middle, and high school instruction. The following section will list the ten themes, explain each one briefly, and give an example within the context of K-6 instruction of how the theme might play out in either an elementary or a middle school classroom.

1. **Culture**—Social studies programs expose students to different cultures: the political, economic, religious, social, intellectual, artistic, and technological advances of distinct groups of people. In the primary grades, students learn about similarities and differences between cultures. Upper elementary students in grades 5–6 begin to explore cultures and ask questions about them.

2. **Time, community, and change**—Social studies programs should emphasize that human beings evolve over time and that history is told by individuals who may hold different views of the past. Older students begin to study American and World history more concretely.

3. **People, places, and environments**—Social studies programs should emphasize geography by exposing younger students to its wide-ranging concepts and skills. This will include attention to how human behavior affects the environment, such as water and air pollution, logging, deforestation, global warming, and ozone layer depletion. As students get older, their ability to abstractly conceptualize about these topics allows teachers to challenge them to analyze situations.

4. **Individual development and identity**—Social studies programs should allow students to learn about how individuals develop within cultural contexts that are unique to them. Younger students may develop this knowledge in the context of their families, peers, and school experiences. Older students learn to relate the individual to the society and culture he or she is from and to make comparisons between cultures.

5. **Individuals, groups, and institutions**—Social studies programs look at interactions between individuals, groups, and institutions like schools, churches, families, courts, and agencies. Younger students should begin to recognize institutions and how they can be in conflict with the individual and with one another. Older learners should see how institutions encourage conformity and change over time.

6. **Power, authority, and governance**—Social studies programs examine issues of power, authority, and governance by examining questions like "What is power?" and "How do governments maintain it?" Younger students develop a sense of fairness and an idea of what their respon-

sibilities are in a particular context. More complex variations of these concepts are employed in the upper levels.

7. **Production, distribution, and consumption**—Social studies programs should examine economic issues such as goods, services, and what is produced, distributed, and consumed within a culture. While younger learners begin to differentiate between needs and wants and to look at their economic experiences in comparison with those of other cultures, older learners begin to use economic reasoning when addressing an issue or problem.

8. **Science, technology, and society**—Social studies programs should examine technology and science in terms of how they impact societal development. Younger learners should be exposed to the notion of how technological progress impacts their lives. Older students can begin to look at the relationships that exist between technology and values.

9. **Global connections**—Social studies programs should be global in focus and should look at tensions between national and global concerns. This analysis transcends fields such as environmentalism, human rights, health care, economic opportunity, etc.

10. **Civic ideals and practices**—Social studies programs should study citizenship and what it means to be involved in one's community. Younger students learn to balance individual and group needs within the context of the classroom, while older students begin to see the kinds of civic roles they can assume within the community.

CONCEPTS IN K-6 SOCIAL STUDIES INSTRUCTION

The following table describes typical topics that are generally covered in each grade (K-6) in social studies:

Table 4.1 K-6 Content Development in Social Studies

K- Grade1	Family, home, school
Grade 2	Community
Grade 3	State history and geography, holidays and history of the United States
Grade 4	Regions of the world or state history/geography
Grade 5	American history and American geography

Grade 6	World history and geography

If one examines the chart holistically, one can see that the content in social studies develops as the student grows and develops. In other words, the curriculum expands as students become more aware of the outside world. Wood (2005) calls this the "widening horizons" approach, which refers to how younger children study from the perspective of personal experience while older students begin to look at information in terms of how it extends beyond themselves.

Still, beyond these general guidelines, what specific content should social studies teachers know about in order to effectively engage their students? The following sections of geography, American history, world history, political science, economics, anthropology, sociology, and psychology are intended to provide an overall context for this important and manifold curriculum. As students of the 0012 exam, you are strongly encouraged to explore these areas in much greater depth in an effort to prepare for the test.

Geography

The Geography Education National Implementation Project (2009) presented eighteen standards for grades K–4 and 5–8. They divided those standards into the following categories: the world in spatial terms; places and regions; physical systems; human systems; the environment and society; and uses of geography.

First and foremost, teachers of social studies need to understand and explain the world spatially. This means teaching students about different kinds of maps: **physical maps** show land and water formations, mountains, and plain. **Cultural maps** show patterns in terms of ethnicities, religions, and languages. **Political maps** show human-made divisions of borders, cities, and towns, while **topographic maps** show roads, train tracks, and bridges. **Weather maps** show temperature and cold fronts. You should know about how mapmakers use **map projections** based on the **geographic grid** (the lines of **latitude** and **longitude** on the globe). You need to know about the **equator,** the **prime meridian (at 0 degrees longitude)** and the **international date line** at 180° longitude. Teachers must show students how to read the parts of a map.

In the sample map (Figure 4.2) on the next page, students should be aware of the **title,** the cardinal **directions (North, South, East, and West)** as indicated by the **compass,** and the **map index** that lists places and coordinates. The students must also become familiar with the **coordinates**, the **key,** the map **grid** (how you read it given the coordinates).

Figure 4.2 Sales Regions

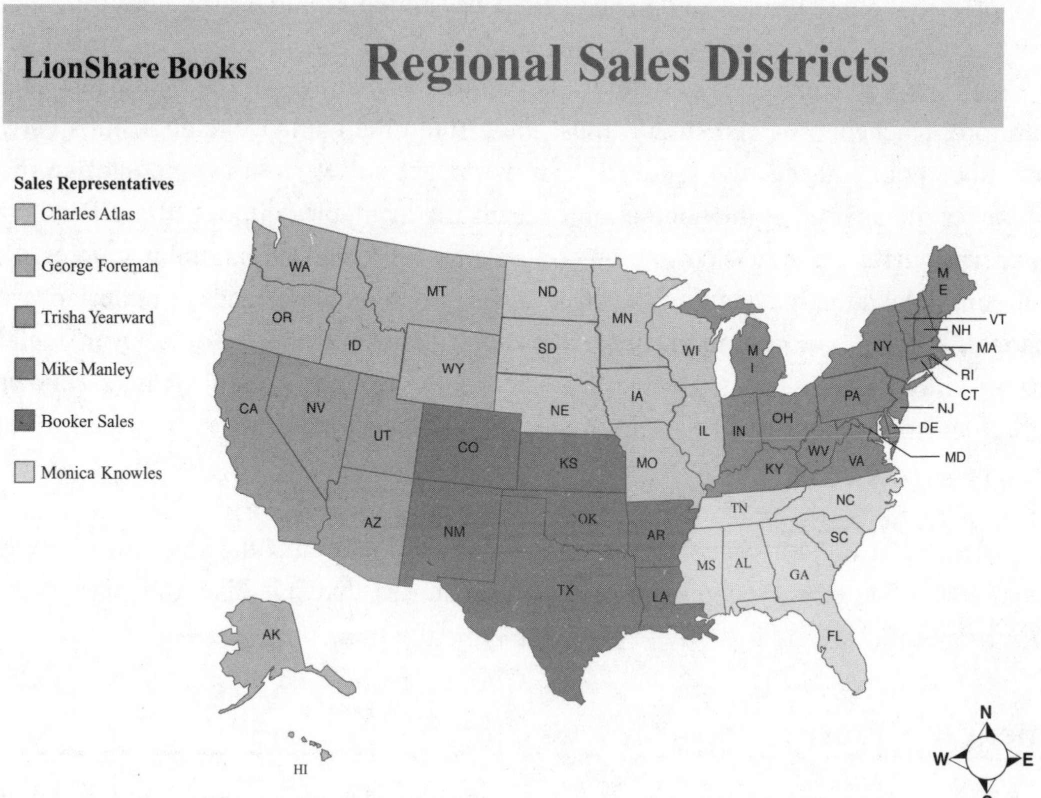

LionShare Books   **Regional Sales Districts**

Sales Representatives
- Charles Atlas
- George Foreman
- Trisha Yearward
- Mike Manley
- Booker Sales
- Monica Knowles

Additionally, the K–6 social studies teacher needs to instruct students about the natural geographic features of the earth: things like **continents, oceans** (Atlantic, Pacific, Indian, and Arctic), **seas,** major **rivers, bays, mountains, plateaus, ice caps**, and **tundra**; and how they compare to human-made features like fields, roads, and landfills. Teachers must also address how borders are categorized in terms of **political, physical,** and **cultural maps** and **divisions**.

The teacher also needs to know about **weather** (the measured conditions of the earth in a particular place and time) versus **climate** (the usual pattern of weather). The teacher must be able to explain certain **physical changes** to the earth like **floods, droughts, snowstorms, earthquakes, glaciers,** and **erosion**.

Geography also includes an understanding of **population trends** in the United States, particularly in the 19th and 20th centuries when millions of immigrants came from Europe, predominantly during the first decade of the 20th century. Generally, individuals immigrate because they are leaving problems like poverty, overcrowding, unemployment, and political oppression to find more economic and educational opportunities as well as tolerance.

Finally, a key concept in geography is the **environment** and how it impacts society. Therefore, teachers of social studies must understand the complex relationships between human behavior and the environment. As a world, we suffer from **overpopulation** in certain places, meaning that the population exceeds the available supplies of food and water. **Conservationists** are interested in protecting plants, animals, and natural resources. Other important areas in understanding the environment include **water** and **air pollution, waste disposal, logging, deforestation, desertification, global warming, ozone layer depletion** (due to chlorofluorocarbons given off by refrigerators and aerosol sprays), **renewable** (i.e. replenished naturally, like solar power) vs. **non-renewable** (not replenished, like oil) **resources**, and **ecosystems**.

Generally, geography is very important because it integrates the study of places with an understanding of the people, cultures, and histories that inhabit those places. It is a much more diverse field of study than people typically think.

American History

When considering U.S. history, one can first consider the exploration and colonization by Europeans leading up to the American Revolution. Clearly, North America was a very different place 30,000 years ago when the first Americans began to arrive over a land bridge that connected Asia and North America. The groups of Native Americans who lived in **nations** had their own cultures and settled all across the region. Explorers from France (**Champlain** and **Cartier**), the Netherlands (**Cabot**), England (**Hudson**), and Spain (**Coronado, Cortes, De Soto, Balboa,** and **Columbus**) explored the northern and central regions of the Americas. They were looking for a new passage to the Far East, for treasure, and for new land. When the first settlers came over and resided in what became the British colonies, they lived in small towns, on farms, and on plantations (in the South). In the New England colonies, fishing and whaling were sources of income, and one cannot forget the religious intolerance of the Puritans, as demonstrated in the Salem witch trials. In the middle Atlantic colonies, settlers raised grain and cattle. Settlers such as William Penn also championed religious freedom. The Southern colonies relied upon slaves to harvest tobacco and cotton. Indeed, the unreconciled differences between the Northern and Southern economies were among the important factors that set the stage for the Civil War.

Disagreements between the colonies and Great Britain began to arise, chiefly because the British Parliament levied many taxes that the colonists had to pay without having any representation in their government. Specifically, Parliament passed the **Proclamation Act of 1763**, which told the colonists they couldn't settle in the lands west of the Appalachian Mountains; the **Stamp Act of 1765**, which made colonists pay tax on things printed on paper; and the **Townshend Acts of 1767**, which not only taxed lead, glass, paper, paint, and tea but also caused the colonists to oppose the Crown. As a result of boycotting by the colonists, the British lifted the taxes on everything except the tea.

In 1768, British soldiers ("redcoats") moved into Boston. Tensions between the soldiers and the colonists resulted in the **Boston Massacre**, an event in 1768 in which soldiers shot and killed five colonists, the first of whom was African-American **Crispus Atticus**. In 1773, the colonists (dressed as Native Americans) boarded ships from the British East India company and dumped the tea into Boston Harbor, an event which became known as the **Boston Tea Party**. As a result, the British passed even tougher regulations which the colonists called the **Intolerable Acts** which, among other things, closed Boston Harbor and forced the colonists to house British troops. This spurred colonial leaders to meet in Philadelphia in September of 1774 at the **First Continental Congress**. All of these events led to the **American Revolution**, the war in which the colonists overthrew the rule of the British and established their own democratic government.

A **Second Continental Congress** met in Philadelphia in May of 1775, and George Washington was commissioned to be the supreme commander of the army. The Second Continental Congress also chose a committee that included Thomas Jefferson, Benjamin Franklin, and John Adams to write what came to be known as the **Declaration of Independence**, signed on July 4, 1776. The main idea of the document was to explain why the colonists were justified in breaking away from England and to describe how the colonists wanted to form a new nation. The document famously asserted that "all men are created equal. . .(and) that they are endowed with certain unalienable rights . . . (such as) life, liberty, and the pursuit of happiness."

In 1781, the **Articles of Confederation** were written and served as the first working document for the new government. In May of 1787, delegates met at the first **Constitutional Convention**. The resulting document, the **Constitution**, laid out the federal government with a **legislative branch**, an **executive branch,** and a **judicial branch**. According to the **system of checks and balances**, no one branch should ever have too much power and each branch has its own authority: the Congress makes laws, the president enforces them, and the court interprets the constitutionality of the laws. The Constitution was ratified in 1788. Nevertheless, some individuals feared that the Constitution would give too much power to a central government, similar to the power that King George of England had; therefore, the **Bill of Rights**, the first Ten Amendments to the Constitution, were added in 1791. The first president, **George Washington**, was elected in 1789. Two major political parties emerged: the **Federalists** (under **John Adams**, who became the second president) and the **Democratic-Republicans** (soon to be known as the "Democrats," under **Thomas Jefferson**, who was elected the third president).

As America expanded westward, certain issues arose. For instance, hundreds of thousands of Africans were captured and brought to the Americas on slave ships, mostly to work on southern plantations. The slave trade increased due to Eli Whitney's invention of the **cotton gin** in 1793. This device pulled out the seeds from the cotton and increased the demand for labor to pick it. America was expanding due to the **Louisiana Purchase**, a huge territory stretching from the Mississippi river to the Rocky Mountains, bought from **Napoleon Bonaparte** (then the Emperor of France) for $15 million in 1803 by **James Madison**, Thomas Jefferson's Secretary of State. In the early 1800s, **Lewis and Clark** explored this territory, and with the assistance of their Native American guide, **Sacajawea**, they eventually reached the Pacific Ocean. The U.S. also had to deal with outside pressures from other nations, like England and France, which were taking U.S. ships in what was known as **impressment.** As a result, the **War of 1812** was waged. Two years later, peace was reached when the **Treaty of Ghent** was signed. By 1823, America had become confident enough to assert that there would be consequences for interfering with the U.S.: the **Monroe Doctrine**, issued by President Monroe, barred European nations from colonizing North or South America.

Between 1800 and 1850, more and more people were moving westward, and many of them traveled across the frontiers of the **Oregon Trail** and the **Santa Fe Trail**. These pioneers journeyed on wagons or on horseback. Sadly, Native Americans were forced by the U.S. government (under President Jackson) to relocate to Oklahoma, and many died or were exposed to diseases on this expedition, which came to be known as the **Trail of Tears**. During this time, a postal system connecting certain cities came about—it was called the **Pony Express**. Meanwhile, in the Southern areas of what we now know as the United States, Mexico gained independence from Spain, and some settlers moved into Texas, which set up its own government under **Sam Houston**. The resulting battle between the Mexican dictator **Santa Anna** and the settlers at the **Alamo**, a Spanish mission that had been overtaken by settlers, ended in a massacre of the settlers, hence the slogan

"Remember the Alamo." When Houston's army captured Santa Anna, he agreed to sign a treaty declaring that Texas was independent. However, the lingering tensions in Mexico from this and other territorial disputes led to the **Mexican War**, which was waged between 1846 and 1848. The U.S. president at this time was **James Polk** who adhered to the doctrine of **Manifest Destiny**, the notion that it was God's will that the U.S. extend from the Atlantic to the Pacific. In the end, Mexico gave up much of its control over the lands that are now known as Arizona, New Mexico, and Colorado. America's expansion was fueled by new forms of transportation like the **steam locomotive**, first invented in 1830 by Robert Fulton. After its inception, many Americans toiled to build tracks across the United States. The **Transcontinental Railroad** was eventually completed in 1869, and this allowed for greater opportunities to travel from coast to coast, thus unifying the nation.

In the mid-1800s, the nation became divided over the issue of **slavery**. The economies of the North and South were different, in that the North was made up of smaller farms and factories with wheat fields which benefited from mechanized harvesting methods, while the South was made up of plantations, with cotton harvesting that required hand labor. Consequently, the economy of the South needed slaves to support it. Certain individuals, known as **abolitionists**, came to feel that slavery was wrong, and they wrote about their ideas in newspaper articles. Some of the more famous abolitionists included **John Brown**, who organized an attack in **Harper's Ferry**, Virginia, in which he planned to give weapons to slaves (he was caught and killed for this act); **Lucretia Mott**, who was also a leader in the women's suffrage movement; **Frederick Douglass**, an escaped slave and journalist; **Harriet Beecher Stowe**, author of *Uncle Tom's Cabin*; and **Harriet Tubman**, who led other slaves to freedom along the **Underground Railroad**, an informal network of secret routes and safe houses to reach the North. During this time leading up to the Civil War, certain compromises were made between the South and the North. For instance, the **Missouri Compromise** allowed Missouri to enter the Union as a slave state insofar as Maine entered as a free state and also insofar as the new lands gained in the Louisiana Purchase disallowed slavery. Similarly, under the **Compromise of 1850**, California entered the Union as a free state and each state in the new Southwestern Territory had to decide for itself if it was a slave or free state. An important debate emerged about a slave named **Dred Scott**, who moved with his owners from a slave to a free state, and thus claimed his freedom. The Supreme Court ruled that as a runaway slave, he was mere chattel or property, with no rights as a citizen.

A new Republican political leader named **Abraham Lincoln** emerged. In his 1858 Senate race, he was engaged in a series of debates with the Democratic Senator Stephen

Douglas. Lincoln eventually lost the Senate race, but their dialogues about slavery put him on the map, and he was elected president in 1860. Lincoln didn't want slavery to be introduced to new states, and he wanted to keep the Union together. Nevertheless, eleven states from the south (South Carolina, Mississippi, Florida, Alabama, Georgia, Louisiana, Texas, Arkansas, North Carolina, Virginia, and Tennessee) seceded, elected **Jefferson Davis** as their president, and formed their own **confederate government**. The **Civil War**, which took place between 1861 and 1865, was fought over the issue of slavery and whether the southern states had the right to secede from the Union. **Ulysses Grant** would eventually lead the Union army, while **Robert E. Lee** commanded the Confederate troops. While the war was fought mainly in the South, the North had more soldiers, more money, and more factories to manufacture weapons. Lincoln issued his **Emancipation Proclamation** as an **Executive Order** in September of 1862, which took effect January 1, 1863. The war ended when Lee surrendered to Grant at **Appomattox** on April 9, 1865. Five days later, Lincoln was assassinated by John Wilkes Booth. Overall, the war caused 620,000 deaths, restored the Union, and strengthened the role of the federal government.

The period after the war came to be known as the **Reconstruction**. This was President Andrew Johnson's major effort to rebuild the Union. In 1865, the **Thirteenth Amendment** freed the slaves; in 1868, the **Fourteenth Amendment** overturned the Dred Scott decision and awarded citizenship to slaves; and in 1869 the **Fifteenth Amendment** gave black men the right to vote. Reassimilation back into the Union happened unevenly in the South, and the Congress during this time imposed military rule there. Likewise, many Northerners called **carpetbaggers** moved to the South to take advantage of the disorder. Still, racism pervaded many areas of the South. The **Ku Klux Klan**, a confederate group that was formed in Tennessee in 1866, burned the homes of blacks, lynched them, and used other means of intimidation to terrorize them. Members of the Klan dressed in white robes with hoods to conceal their identities. **Jim Crow laws**, passed in Southern states to legalize segregation, created "separate but equal" areas. The idea of "separate but equal" stems from the 1896 Supreme Court case, **Plessy v. Ferguson**, which made segregation legal.

The **Industrial Revolution**, a movement which began in Great Britain in the 1760s, later spread to the United States. It changed the way people earned money, with a transition from farming and fishing to working in coal, iron, and steel factories. Much of this transformation is credited to technological innovations like the **steam engine**, the **spinning jenny**, the **power loom**, and the **cotton gin**. Moreover, people flocked to cities to gain employment.

As the nation headed towards the end of the 1800s, an age of monopolies emerged in the north. Big businesses run by industrialists like John D. **Rockefeller** (oil), Cornelius **Vanderbilt** (railroads), Andrew **Carnegie** (steel), and William Randolph **Hearst** and Joseph **Pulitzer** (newspapers) controlled specific markets. Other leaders who emerged during this time were inventors—this list includes Alexander Graham **Bell**, who invented the telephone; Thomas **Edison**, who invented the light bulb; and Henry **Ford**, who developed the first car.

Under President McKinley, the United States was dealing with another war, the **Spanish American War** of 1898: Cuba was fighting for independence from Spain. When the U.S. battleship *Maine* went to Cuba and exploded, the Hearst newspapers contended that it occurred because the Spanish perceived that the U.S. was supporting Cuba and blew up the ship. As a result, McKinley declared war on Spain and began fighting in the Philippines, which was a Spanish colony. Under then military leader Teddy Roosevelt, the U.S. cavalry fought the Battle of San Juan in Cuba. The U.S. won this war and gained control of Cuba as well as the Spanish colonies of Puerto Rico, Guam, and the Philippines.

PRAXIS Pointer

When you feel anxious, close your eyes, and take a couple of long, deep breaths. Then hold it and exhale slowly. Imagine a peaceful place to visit.

Back in the U.S., the Industrial Revolution was providing many employment opportunities, but there were few safeguards in place at the factories, which were often overcrowded and unsanitary. **Muckrakers** (journalists who spoke up against abuses) and progressives spoke out against these injustices. Upton Sinclair's 1906 book *The Jungle* exposed these abuses. As the first pieces of legislation regulating child labor and working conditions were passed in England, the movement spread here. Labor unions eventually formed, and (after McKinley was assassinated) then Vice President **Theodore Roosevelt** became president. Roosevelt was a progressive "trust buster" who passed legislation like the **Sherman Anti-Trust Act** to break up the monopolies. He was famous for his slogan, "Speak softly and carry a big stick."

The twentieth century ushered in an age of transformation when it came to women's rights, war, artistic expression, economic frailty, and technological development. Similar to the abolitionists, women fought for their rights as far back as the 1800s when **suffragists** like **Elizabeth Cady Stanton** and **Lucretia Mott** organized the first women's rights convention in Seneca Falls, NY. Similarly, **Susan B. Anthony** fought for women's right to vote. The struggle continued into the beginning of the twentieth century. As the movement gained in popularity, suffragists were arrested and jailed. Finally, President **Woodrow Wilson** urged Congress to pass what became, when it was ratified in 1920, the **Nineteenth Amendment**, giving women the right to vote.

In Europe, countries formed alliances to increase their sizes and influences. For instance, Germany, Austria-Hungary, and Italy signed the **Triple Alliance** while France, Russia, and England formed the **Triple Entente**. When Ferdinand, the Archduke of Austria, was assassinated in Sarajevo (in Serbia), Austria-Hungary attacked Serbia and, in response countries joined either alliance. The United States initially sought neutrality (in that it could profit by being the arms dealer to both sides), but eventually German submarine warfare and heavier export trade to England caused the U.S. to declare war against Germany. The pivotal moment was when the Germans sank a British passenger ship called the *Lusitania*. In 1917, when American ships were continually sunk by the Germans, President Wilson petitioned Congress to declare war on Germany. When World War I was finally over, the **Treaty of Versailles** was signed, forcing Germany to give up land and colonies to France, Belgium, Denmark, and Poland. Germany also had to reduce its military and pay millions in reparations, or damages, to other nations.

In some areas of the U.S., the 1920s could be characterized as the **Roaring Twenties**; art and music were thriving and many people speculated in and benefited from the stock market. In one neighborhood of New York City, the **Harlem Renaissance** was born which was fostered by jazz musicians like Duke Ellington and writers like Langston Hughes. But this age of happiness was short-lived. Over-speculation in the market, frivolous loans made by banks, and an over-reliance on stocks all led to the stock market crash of 1929, when many companies went bankrupt, people lost their jobs and were unable to pay back loans, and thousands of banks closed. The resulting massive unemployment was a huge crisis for the nation and a task taken on by President **Franklin Delano Roosevelt**. Elected in 1932, Roosevelt initiated his **New Deal** which introduced innovative programs like the Tennessee Valley Authority and the Civilian Conservation Corps; these initiatives served to create jobs for Americans. FDR's administration also activated **Social Security**.

During this time, a sense of extremism and uncompromising fanaticism was taking hold in Japan (**Hirohito**), Italy (**Mussolini**), and most especially Germany (**Adolf Hitler**). This mood of **reactionism** was caused by the combined results of the **Great Depression** and the humiliation brought on by the Treaty of Versailles. **Hitler** rose to power and began realizing his desire to conquer the world. In World War II, each of these three aligned

Axis countries invaded neighboring lands. Initially, the United States took an isolationist stance regarding the war. However, when the Japanese bombed the U.S. Naval base at **Pearl Harbor**, Hawaii, in December of 1941, the U.S. declared war on the Axis powers and joined the **Allies** (France, England, and the Soviet Union in addition to other, smaller countries). During WWII, Hitler tried to achieve supremacy for what he believed should be an **Aryan race** of white people by killing people he considered to be undesirables, at first in ghettos and then in concentration camps. While some camps served as work prisons, many were actual death factories where more than 11 million people (6 million of whom were Jews, the others being gypsies, disabled people, homosexuals, and opponents of the Nazis) were exterminated in a massive **genocide**. The Italians and Germans eventually surrendered to the Allies in 1945. The Japanese, unwilling to surrender, did so after **two atomic bombs** were dropped on **Hiroshima** and **Nagasaki** in August of 1945. These bombs were developed in a secret undertaking called the **Manhattan Project**.

As a result of World War II, Germany was subdivided into East and West, the Soviet Union continued to dominate occupied countries in Eastern Europe, and the **United Nations**, a body designed to maintain peace and security in the world, was instituted in 1945. Two other wars that took place during the second half of the twentieth century were the **Korean War** (1950–1953) and the **Vietnam War** (1957–1975). In both cases, the U.S. supported the southern portion of the countries (South Korea and South Vietnam, respectively) in response to the hazards posed by the invasive and Communist-ruled northern portions. Whereas in Korea the North and South remained separated at war's end, in Vietnam the entire country was reunified under the control of Communist rule. The threat of nuclear war continued to be made evident by the **Cold War** that ensued between U.S. and the Soviet Union, who had been allies only a generation earlier.

Other noteworthy events happened in the mid-twentieth century as well. **Martin Luther King Jr**., a non-violent protester, and **Malcolm X**, a leader who espoused more militant approaches, both rose to power as advocates for African American rights. The **Civil Rights movement** (beginning with *Brown v. Board of Education* in 1954) ushered in important legislation that encouraged an end to the segregation and racial discrimination that still existed in the U.S. The **Persian Gulf War** (1991–1992) was the multinational effort to expel Iraq from Kuwait after it had been invaded. In more recent history, Europe adopted a common currency, the **Euro**, in 1992 in an effort to bring together the countries of Europe. The **Internet** ushered in a culture of globalism and intellectual trade which is currently spoken of when we consider the "**global economy**."

Major events at the beginning of the twenty-first century included the terrorist attacks on New York City and Washington, D.C., by Osama bin Laden and Al Qaeda on **September 11, 2001**, the wars in **Afghanistan** and **Iraq**, and the inauguration of the first African American U.S. president, Barack Obama, on January 20, 2009.

World History

When considering world history, one must first consider pre-history and early civilizations. The **Paleolithic** and **Neolithic periods** were characterized by a move away from nomadic life towards domestication. Many people lived in hunter-gatherer societies, meaning that they would fish and hunt for food. Slowly, humans learned to farm. It is significant that many major societies settled around bodies of water. For instance, our most ancient civilization, **Mesopotamia**, was founded between two rivers, the **Tigris** and the **Euphrates**. The **Sumerians** were one of the first people to live on this fertile land, from 3500–2000 BCE. They were the founders of modern civilization in that they developed an alphabet (**cuneiform**), had an army with weapons, studied math and science, made vehicles with wheels, and had a society with three classes (wealthy, working class, and slaves). Alongside the Sumerians, the **Babylonians** built their city, Babylon, on the Euphrates around 2000 BCE Subsequent civilizations established in this area included the **Assyrians** (circa 1350 BCE), the **Hebrews** (who left Egypt and eventually settled in Palestine around 1000 BCE), the **Phoenicians** (who lived along the Mediterranean around 1000 BCE), the **Persians** (circa 500 BCE), and the **Hittites** (who lived near Turkey from 1700–1200 BCE)

Other early civilizations emerged in India (near the Indus River valley from 3000–1500 BCE), China (around the Yellow and Long rivers, around 2000 BCE), and Mesoamerica (in what is now known as Mexico and Central America, by the Aztec, Olmec, and Mayan people from 1200 BCE-400 BCE). Of course, the **Mayans** started one of the most sophisticated civilizations, one which utilized calendars, math, astronomy, and architecture, particularly pyramids. After the Mayans, the **Aztecs** established the city of **Tenochtitlan** which had well-engineered roads and waterways. In 1519, the Aztec emperor **Montezuma** was defeated by the Spanish explorer **Cortes**, who destroyed Tenochtitlan and called the new city Mexico City. Civilizations were also growing in South America, and one of the most famous was the **Incan** empire. Like many of the other civilizations, the Incans developed a mathematics system. They also were very skilled architects who carved out a beautiful city called **Machu Picchu**. When the Spanish conquistador **Pizarro** landed there, he and some Spanish soldiers took over the empire, and it became part of Spain.

It is important to understand the classical civilizations of Egypt, Greece, and Rome in order to realize how civilization advanced in these ancient times. **Egypt** (2700 BCE– 30 BCE) was founded near the Nile River. The Egyptians were advanced in that they developed a language (**hieroglyphics**), made paper, created a calendar, and built pyramids (which were tombs for the pharaohs). They were ruled by numerous dynasties and many famous royals such as King Tutankhamen and Cleopatra.

Around the same time period, the **Greeks** were living in southern Europe. Their land was divided into **city-states** (where each city had self-rule), the earliest and most powerful of which were Athens and Sparta. Athens became the first democracy, and it was characterized by voting by male citizens. On the other hand, Sparta was dominated by military rule. The two cities eventually went to war in 431 BCE This war, called the **Peloponnesian War**, lasted for 27 years and resulted in victory for Sparta. After this war, King Philip II of Macedonia took over the destabilized city-states, and his son Alexander (who became known as **Alexander the Great**) expanded the Greek empire from what is now Greece to lands much further east, eventually all the way to what is now India. While Alexander wanted to bring together all of the people in these lands, his plan was cut short when he died. Still, Ancient Greece is a significant civilization because of the great contributions that were made by (to name a few) philosophers like **Socrates, Plato,** and **Aristotle**; gods (like Zeus, Aphrodite, and Apollo); the Olympics; medicine (Hippocrates); mathematics (Euclid); drama (Euripides and Sophocles); literature (the *Illiad* and the *Odyssey*); architecture (Greek columns); and sculpture.

In contrast, ancient **Rome** began in an area of southern Europe on the Tiber River and expanded gradually. Rome was conquered and ruled by the Etruscans from 750–500 BCE, when the people revolted and created a republic. The citizens of Rome ran the government, and men who were not slaves were allowed to vote. There were two classes: the patricians (wealthy) and the plebeians (working class). Rome eventually grew because its emperors (rulers such as Julius Caesar; his son, Caesar Augustus; Hadrian; and Marcus Aurelius) invaded areas such as Italy, Greece, the lands by the Mediterranean Sea, and Carthage (in North Africa, which the Romans won as a result of the Punic Wars in 146 BCE). Nevertheless, the Roman Empire began to decline in 180 CE because it had grown too large, and it was too difficult to control and finance. The Huns, or barbarians, invaded and eventually conquered Rome around 400 CE. Rome was important because of the many accomplishments that took place there: Romans had their own gods (like Jupiter, Venus, and Neptune); they built roads, bridges, arches, columns, and important buildings like the Pantheon and the Colosseum; their language (Latin) became the source for many other romance languages; they had their own famous literature (the *Aeneid*); and they devised the system of Roman numerals.

Other non-European civilizations are important to understand when one considers world history. For instance, the **Muslim Empire**, founded by the prophet Muhammad around 650 CE, was characterized by the spread of Islam throughout Spain, North Africa, Egypt, Arabia, and Persia. Muhammad's teachings were written down in the Islamic holy book, the *Qur'an*—which tells its followers to worship no god but Allah, to pray five times a day, to treat others as brothers and sisters, to give to the poor, to fast during the holy month of Ramadan, and to make a pilgrimage at least once in one's life to Mecca.

In addition, early civilization in **India** (3000–1500 BCE) began in the area along the Indus River valley. The religion of India was Hinduism, and, in contrast to Islam, it was characterized by multiple gods and goddesses. Hinduism's sacred text, the *Upanishads*, was written around 400 BCE and speaks of a Brahman, one great Being, as well as the self or soul, called Atman. Hindus accept the idea of reincarnation, the notion that one living thing passes on into the life of another as opposed to just dying. In India, there was a caste system whereby people were divided into four groups: priests, warriors, workpeople, and peasants/servants. Those who did not fall into any of the groups were called "untouchables."

Another religion which began in India and eventually spread to China and Japan was **Buddhism**. A young boy named Siddhartha gave sermons and eventually became known as the Buddha, or enlightened one. The religion emphasized bringing an end to unequal treatment of others, embracing a life of love, and increasing overall joy by ending all desires. In ancient India, temples were constructed, literature was written using Sanskrit, and sacred Hindu texts like the *Bhagavad Gita* were composed. Other advances were made during the Golden Age of India (around 500 CE) when Arabic numerals and decimals were devised. This age came to an end when the Muslims invaded their lands between 1000 and 1500 CE. The Muslims dominated the Indians in terms of government, religion, language (Arabic and Persian replaced Hindi and eventually were blended together to become what is now known as Urdu), and buildings. Eventually, India became a colony of the British, and it wasn't until **Gandhi** called for passive resistance against the British that India eventually succeeded in gaining self-rule in 1947.

Similar to India, **China** was a civilization that grew alongside rivers—the Yellow and the Long rivers. China was characterized by dynasties ruled by emperors from 2000 BCE. to 1910 CE. In addition to Buddhism, their other major religion was **Confucianism**, and emerged from Confucius (551–479 BCE), who taught people to live a virtuous life. Another religion, **Taoism**, was founded by a contemporary of Confucius, Lao-tzu, who taught people to meditate and appreciate nature in order to achieve inner peace. China was no longer run by dynasties as of 1911, when a revolution led by **Sun Yat-sen** made China a republic. Sun Yat-sen became the first president of China, and then eventually China came under control of the Communists under the leadership of **Mao Zedong**.

It is also important to consider the development of **Japan**, where shoguns and samurai warriors fought for their lords and emperors under a system of feudalism. Civil wars persisted in Japan until 1600, when **Tokugawa** took power, expelled foreigners from Japan, outlawed Christianity, and started a period of isolation that would last until 1853, when **Commodore Matthew Perry** of the U.S. established trade with the Japanese. Then, under the Meiji leaders, Japan became more Westernized. In fact, Japan experienced the most rapid and successful industrialization of a country in history.

Finally, another region characterized by empires was **Africa**. Specifically, empires existed in Ghana, Mali, Songhai, and Zimbabwe. While these empires made great advances in terms of trade and commerce, within the Age of Exploration much of Africa was colonized by six European countries: France, Great Britain, Portugal, Germany, Belgium, and Italy. Many of these areas have only recently been decolonized. Specifically, Kenya, Angola, and Mozambique gained independence in the 1960s and 1970s, while South Africa and Namibia declared self-rule as recently as the 1980s and 1990s. The result of this decolonization has been an overall instability in Africa that still exists today.

During the **Middle Ages** (roughly 400–1500 CE), a feudal system with three classes of people (nobles, clergy, and peasants) defined what European society was like. Around 1350, a terrible disease known as the plague or **Black Death** spread throughout Europe and killed about one-third of all Europeans in the course of three years. Right around this time, the **Renaissance** was spreading from northern Italy throughout Europe. It was a rebirth of art, literature, science, and technology that celebrated the individual and rejected feudalism. **Michelangelo** (the *David* and the *Pieta*), **da Vinci** (the *Mona Lisa* and *The Last Supper*), **Machiavelli** (*The Prince*), and **Guttenberg** (who invented the printing press) are just a few of the big names to come out of the Renaissance. The **Protestant Reformation**, a revolt against the Roman Catholic Church led by German preacher **Martin Luther**, followed the Renaissance. For many, the Catholic Church had become too powerful, and many people resented having to pay taxes and indulgences (money for favors) to them. Luther posted his list of complaints, the **Ninety-Five Theses**, to the door of a Catholic church in Wittenberg, Germany. After he was excommunicated by the pope, he started his own religion, the Lutherans. Similar movements away from Catholicism formed within Protestantism (such as the **Calvinists**, who were the original Presbyterians, and the **Anglicans**, a movement founded because England's King Henry VIII wanted a divorce and the pope wouldn't allow it). The Catholics fought back with their own reformation, known as the **Counter-Reformation**, in which they set up **Inquisition** courts to try Protestants and those of other faiths. Catholics also began missionary efforts to stop people from converting to Protestantism.

As was previously mentioned in the American history section, Europe was expanding due to the **Age of Exploration** which began in Europe and took place between the late 1400s and the early 1600s. Explorers from Spain like **Coronado, De Soto, Balboa,** and **Columbus** were discovering what is now Mexico and Central America, while others from France (**Cartier and Champlain**), the Netherlands (**Cabot**) and England (**Hudson**) were tackling North America. **Magellan** of Spain became the first explorer to sail around the world, while **Da Gama** (Portugal) was the first to sail around Africa's Cape of Good Hope and reach India from Europe by sea. **Marco Polo** was able to reach India and China by land. Explorers were looking to establish new trade paths, find riches, gain colonies, and spread Christianity. French explorers claimed the land from Canada over to the Great Lakes and Mississippi, and they called this **New France**; the British initially controlled the eastern section of what is now the United States (the **thirteen original colonies**); and the Spanish explorers took the land all along the south from Florida to California and down to Panama, calling it **New Spain**.

In the early 1700s, Renaissance ideas and the thoughts of the **Scientific Revolution** emerged into a new understanding called the **Enlightenment**. With ideas that fueled the American and French revolutions, philosophers like **Locke, Voltaire, Montesquieu,** and **Rousseau** talked about individual rights. Indeed, it was during the **French Revolution** (1789) that citizens rejected the ruling system in France of the "three estates" (the Church, the nobles, and the commoners). French citizens stormed the **Bastille** (an ammunition warehouse), beheaded aristocrats using the guillotine, and put forth the **Declaration of the Rights of Man**, written by Lafayette. In 1794, the Revolution ended and the National Assembly and its Constitution dissolved the absolute monarchy of the king. This gave rise to the rule of **Napoleon Bonaparte**, a military leader who came to power in 1799, expanded France's empire, and eventually crowned himself emperor. After Napoleon had managed to overtake much of Europe, several countries joined forces to fight back. In 1815, they were able to defeat him in the **Battle of Waterloo**.

Many of the developments of the twentieth century were previously discussed under "American History." Nevertheless, three important revolutions need to be mentioned. In

Russia and many other countries, industrialism led to social problems among workers. **Karl Marx**, a German philosopher, worked with **Friedrich Engels** to write a book called *The Communist Manifesto*, in which they argued for a better system. Their ideas spread, and in the twentieth century many countries around the world adopted communism as their system of government. For instance, Russia had many upset workers who wanted to see an end to the power of the czar. These workers went on strike and overthrew the Czar (Nicholas II). A man named **Vladimir Lenin** and his Bolsheviks overthrew the government in the **Russian Revolution**. A civil war was waged and eventually, Lenin formed the Union of Soviet Socialist Republics (USSR) in 1922. The Soviet Union, remained a communist republic until 1990, when the USSR was broken up, individual elections were held in the different regions, and a free market-based economy was embraced.

On the other hand, the **Mexicans**, who had been colonized by the Spanish from the time when Cortes destroyed the Aztecs, began fighting back in the 1800s. Although they lost a lot of land to the U.S., had to battle the French who had invaded their territory, and were ruled by Diaz from 1876 to 1910, they also eventually had a revolution (supported by **Pancho Villa**) in which land was taken from the rich and given to the poor. Ultimately, the revolution ended in 1920, and a new constitution was adopted, establishing Mexico's independence.

A final revolution that distinguished the twentieth century was the **Chinese Revolution**, which brought an end to the rule of dynasties and ultimately led to communist rule in China. Specifically, the communist People's Liberation Army, under the leadership of Mao Zedong, defeated Chiang Kai-shek and declared the region "the People's Republic of China."

Political Science

A given edition of the Praxis 0012 test could very well concern the area of political science as it relates to the United States. Therefore, this section will briefly describe some important areas to review.

The government of the U.S. is laid out in the **Constitution**, the preamble of which reads,

> We the people of the United States, in order to form a more perfect union, establish justice, insure domestic tranquility, provide for the common defense, promote the general welfare, and secure the blessings of liberty to ourselves and our posterity, do ordain and establish this Constitution, for the United States of America.

The preamble introduces the idea that citizens in the U.S. set up their own government in response to being ruled without being represented by England. The Constitution lays out the system of **three branches of government**: the **executive branch** (led by the president, who is elected every four years for no more than two terms, is chief of the Congress and commander of the armed forces, can either sign or veto bills that are passed in the Congress, makes decisions in foreign policy, and makes sure that the laws passed are carried out); the **legislative branch** (the Congress, made up of senators—two from each state who serve a six year term, and representatives from the House of Representatives, whose number is calculated according to population of each state and serve two-year terms); and the **judicial branch**, where (thanks to the the Federal and State courts) judges decide if laws have been broken and if they are constitutional. The final legal arbiters are the U.S. Supreme Court justices, who are appointed by the president and serve lifelong terms.

If the president is unable to serve out his or her term, the power is passed along according to a specific chain of command. First is the Vice President, then the Speaker of the House, then the President Pro Tempore of the Senate (or the highest ranking official of the Senate next to the Vice President, who is in charge of the Senate), then to the Secretary of State. The President has a cabinet which consists of the Vice President and appointees charged with heading other departments: Secretaries of State, Treasury, Defense, Interior, Agriculture, Commerce, Labor, Health and Human Services, Housing and Urban Development, Transportation, Energy, Education, Veterans Affairs, and Homeland Security, plus the U.S. Attorney General.

It is important to understand **how a bill becomes a law**. A bill may start in either the House or the Senate. It is introduced by a representative or senator, and it is sent to the proper committee, where it is discussed and possibly changed after hearings are held regarding it. If it is approved, it goes to the rules committee where it is put on the agenda of the House or the Senate, debated, and voted on. If it passes (say, in the House or the Senate with a simple majority), it then goes to the opposite chamber of Congress. If it doesn't pass there, a committee of House and Senate members works together to redraft and re-present it. If it passes in both chambers, it goes to the president, who has ten days to either sign or veto it. If it is signed, it becomes a law. If it is vetoed, Congress can override that decision by a two-thirds vote of both the House and the Senate.

Voters in each state choose electors for the **Electoral College**. These individuals vote for the president or vice president based on the popular votes cast in each state. The number of electors per state is calculated by adding the number of senators (two) plus the number of representatives in the House (which is based on population). For instance, New York has 29 representatives in the House and two senators, so they have 31 electoral votes. If one calculates the number of House members (435) and adds the number of senators (100), the total is 535; the majority of these electors decide who becomes president. As history has demonstrated, according to this system a candidate can win the popular vote but lose in the Electoral College. For example, in 2000 Al Gore won the popular vote but lost in the Electoral College to George W. Bush.

The Constitution empowers Congress to try a president who is accused of treason, bribery, or another high crime. The House may accuse, or **impeach** this president. The trial is held in the Senate, and if two-thirds of the senators vote against the president, he is convicted and must leave his or her office. Recently, former President **Bill Clinton** was impeached by the House but not convicted by the Senate: thus, he served out the rest of his term. The only other U.S. president to be impeached was **Andrew Johnson**; no president has been convicted by the Senate.

After the Constitution was passed in 1787, certain rights were added to it in 1791. Primarily written by James Madison, these ten rights are called the **Bill of Rights** and they are as follows:

- First Amendment: *Congress shall make no law respecting an establishment of religion, or prohibiting the free exercise thereof; or abridging the freedom of speech, or of the press; or the right of the people peaceably to assemble, and to petition the Government for a redress of grievances.*
- Second Amendment: *A well regulated Militia being necessary to the security of a free State, the right of the people to keep and bear Arms, shall not be infringed.*
- Third Amendment: *No Soldier shall, in time of peace be quartered in any house, without the consent of the Owner, nor in time of war, but in a manner to be prescribed by law.*
- Fourth Amendment: *The right of the people to be secure in their persons, houses, papers, and effects, against unreasonable searches and seizures, shall not be violated, and no warrants shall issue, but upon probable cause, supported by Oath or affirmation, and particularly describing the place to be searched, and the persons or things to be seized.*
- Fifth Amendment: *No person shall be held to answer for any capital, or otherwise infamous crime, unless on a presentment or indictment of a Grand Jury, except in cases arising in the land or naval forces, or in the Militia, when in actual service in time of War or public danger; nor shall any person be subject for the same offence to be twice put in jeop-*

ardy of life or limb; nor shall be compelled in any criminal case to be a witness against himself, nor be deprived of life, liberty, or property, without due process of law; nor shall private property be taken for public use, without just compensation.

- Sixth Amendment: *In all criminal prosecutions, the accused shall enjoy the right to a speedy and public trial, by an impartial jury of the State and district where in the crime shall have been committed, which district shall have been previously ascertained by law, and to be informed of the nature and cause of the accusation; to be confronted with the witnesses against him; to have compulsory process for obtaining witnesses in his favor, and to have the Assistance of Counsel for his defense.*

- Seventh Amendment: *In suits at common law, where the value in controversy shall exceed twenty dollars, the right of trial by jury shall be preserved, and no fact tried by a jury, shall be otherwise re-examined in any court of the United States, than according to the rules of the common law.*

- Eighth Amendment: *Excessive bail shall not be required, nor excessive fines imposed, nor cruel and unusual punishments inflicted.*

- Ninth Amendment: *The enumeration in the Constitution, of certain rights, shall not be construed to deny or disparage others retained by the people.*

- Tenth Amendment: *The powers not delegated to the United States by the Constitution, nor prohibited by it to the states, are reserved to the states respectively, or to the people.*

Additional amendments have been passed over the years, and we currently have **twenty-seven** in all. For instance, the Nineteenth Amendment gave women the right to vote, and the Twenty-sixth Amendment lowered the voting age from 21 to 18.

State governments are similar to the federal government with the exception that each state is led by a governor.

Economics is the social science that studies the production, distribution, and consumption of goods and services. In the tradition of **Adam Smith**, economists view the world through the lens of scarcity, as well as supply and demand. **Scarcity** limits our options and necessitates that we make choices. Because we can't have it all, we must decide what we will have and what we must forego. A **resource** helps produce a good (product) or service (which includes the transfer of goods, like the postal service delivering mail, or a person visiting a dentist). The **market** is any institution or mechanism that brings together buyers (demanders) and sellers (suppliers). The market is the place where goods and services can be bought and sold. **Supply** is a schedule showing the amounts of a good or service that seller will offer at various prices during some period. **Demand** is a schedule showing the amounts of a good or service that buyers wish to purchase at various prices during the same time period. In other words, it is what people will spend to purchase an item. When supply is limited, it increases the demand, and prices go up. This competition to make even more desirable products leads to innovation. Often seen as a synonym for "money," the word **capital** is also used to describe human-made resources (buildings, machinery, and equipment) used to produce goods and services. **Property** is capital, land, stocks, bonds, and other assets owned by firms and households. Overall, economics is a dynamic field within social studies which helps us understand the impact our decisions have on small (micro) and big (macro) levels.

Anthropology is the study of modern-day and prehistoric cultures. Archaeologists like **Richard Leakey** excavate, scientifically analyze, and attempt to reconstruct the lives of extinct peoples. Primatologists like **Dr. Jane Goodall** study the group behavior of primates. Ethnographers like **Margaret Mead** gain information about culture through site-based fieldwork. Linguistic anthropologists study the social context of languages, while physical or biological anthropologists study living human beings and primates. Anthropologists might study issues that affect humankind such as **cultural identity**, **population**, and **ethnology**.

Sociology is the study of human behavior within society. Sociologists study groups such as families, workers, criminals, men, and women. They are intrigued by how groups and institutions interact. They also might consider issues such as **adaptation, assimilation, acculturation, gender roles,** and **human development** in terms of how they impact the overall socialization process.

Psychology is the study of human behavior. **Psychoanalysis**, or the notion of resolving one's unconscious conflicts that arose from childhood traumas, was developed by Sigmund Freud (1890–1939). **Carl Jung** (the collective unconscious and psychological archetypes), **Erik Erikson** (theory of social development) and other twentieth century thinkers came after Freud. **Behavioral psychologists** like **B.F. Skinner** reacted against Freud by arguing that psychology should only be concerned with the study of observable behavior. They relied on research by scientists such as **Ivan Pavlov** who studied classical conditioning in dogs. Individuals like linguist **Noam Chomsky** challenged Skinner's behaviorist approaches in what later became known as **cognitive psychology**, which differs from the other approaches in that it is primarily interested in how people think and learn. **Social psychology** is often credited to **Albert Bandura** thanks to his "social learning theory," which says that people learn through reinforcement, punishment, or observation of the behaviors of others. **Humanist psychology** looks at the whole person by focusing on subjective issues like self-identity, death, aloneness, freedom, and meaning. The leaders in this area of psychology include **Abraham Maslow** (with his hierarchy of human needs), **Carl Rogers** (client centered therapy), and **Fritz Perls** (Gestalt therapy). **Existential psychologists** rely on the work of philosophers **Heidegger** and **Kierkegaard** to help people understand issues like mortality, free will, and choice. **Developmental psychologists** look at psychological changes in an individual over the lifespan. **Educational psychologists** look at how individuals learn in school settings. **Clinical psychologists** study abnormal behavior and promote personal well-being.

INSTRUCTION IN SOCIAL SCIENCES

In discussing the best general practices to use in teaching social studies, Zemelman, Daniels, and Hyde (1998) underscore that teachers should de-emphasize memorization of facts and lecture-based methods. Rather, teachers should encourage in-depth study of topics by including activities that engage students in inquiry, problem solving, decision making, cooperative learning, integration of all aspects of social studies (like history, geography, economics), and comprehension of culture and citizenship. Again, all of these methods are within the overall framework of state curricular standards. Zemelman, Daniels, and Hyde (1998) assert that the best social studies classrooms are:

STUDENT-CENTERED: They investigate the questions of students and allow student input to take precedence over selected content.

EXPERIENTIAL: They have hands-on activities with concrete experiences.

HOLISTIC: They give students whole ideas, events, and materials in purposeful contexts, not by studying sub-parts isolated from actual use.

AUTHENTIC: They utilize complex ideas and materials.

EXPRESSIVE: They engage students by using a range of communication media, including speeches, poems, writing, dance, drama, visual arts, and movement.

REFLECTIVE: They allow students to reflect, debrief, and ponder what they have gained from their learning experiences.

SOCIAL: They respect that learning is socially constructed.

COLLABORATIVE: They use cooperative learning as opposed to individual-istic approaches.

DEMOCRATIC: The classroom is a model community where students behave as citizens of the school.

COGNITIVE: The classroom is an environment where students develop and understand concepts.

DEVELOPMENTAL: The class is geared towards the developmental level of each student.

CONSTRUCTIVIST: Children do not just receive content; in a very real sense, they re-create and re-invent every cognitive system they encounter.

CHALLENGING: Teachers give students authentic challenges, choices, and responsibilities in their own learning.

Keeping these general principles in mind, we will now draw our attention to what we can argue is the central motivation of the elementary school social studies teacher: teaching students how to engage in **systematic inquiry**. In other words, a good social studies teacher consistently shows students how to acquire information from a variety of resources, organize that information, and interpret it. Let's break this definition apart in an effort to understand just what the teacher does.

Acquiring information from a variety of resources: What information are we talking about? Social studies teachers help students navigate

Primary sources (diaries, ledgers, oral histories, census reports, photographs, etc.)

Secondary sources (primarily, the classroom textbook but also encyclopedias, magazine articles, newspaper articles, Internet web pages, etc.)

Organizing that information: How does the teacher arrange the materials to be presented, and what kinds of materials does he or she use?

In addition to the textbook, good social studies teachers incorporate audiovisual aids (videos, software) as well as pri-mary sources, newspaper articles, documentaries, etc. Their classrooms display posters, charts, maps, drawings, and artwork that complement the learning goals. They invite meaningful human resources (community members, historians, librarians, and parents) in to supplement the learning. They take students on field trips where students record real life observations and bring them back into the classroom, and they even teach students about the foods of different regions.

Interpreting the information: How do we assign value to various sources of information? How do we establish a big picture understanding of a topic from various small pieces of data?

Good social studies teachers help students learn how to evaluate primary sources and to gain a historical perspective about them. This might involve having students assess documents, letters, diaries, eyewitness accounts, and photos. Good social studies teachers show students how to detect and decode biases, synthesize various primary sources, and come up with conclusions about documents.

When it comes to **planning units** in social studies, the teacher needs to take into account the name of the unit, the target audience and level, how long it will take to teach, the curricular objectives that need to be met, how those objectives will be assessed, the learning outcomes (what students will be able to do as a result of this unit), the activities that will be used, and the outside resources (books, DVDs, websites, etc.) that will be integrated into the instruction. The unit that is taught should correlate with district, state, and national guidelines for instruction. Lemlech (1994) lists concepts which are typically taught in elementary and middle school classrooms; his list includes acculturation, adaptation, assimilation, behavior, change, communication, community, competition, conflict, cooperation, culture, diversity, family, freedom, government, groups, interdependence, justice, migration, power, rules, scarcity, and socialization.

Teaching by theme helps the teacher bring in all aspects of social studies. In a typical unit, the teacher introduces the theme, builds lessons around it which incorporate activities that foster social studies skills (like gathering data, making inferences, predicting, and detecting bias), and then concludes the unit with an assessment. Kniep (1989) laid out certain conceptual themes that can help shape the units that make up the social studies curriculum. They include: interdependence (how we live in a world of interdependent systems), change (moving from one thing to the next, which includes adaptation, evolution, growth, revolution), culture (the unique political, economic, social, religious, and linguistic environments in which people find themselves), scarcity (imbalance between wants and resources), and conflict (differing values of groups and nations).

One activity that is very important in this context is organizing lessons and whole units around **essential questions**. In essence, these questions help teachers engage students in social science inquiry, whereby the students are gaining in-depth knowledge of important content while they are also learning how to think, question, and make informed decisions. Here is an example of an essential question to use in a fifth grade classroom: "Why is the First Amendment the First Amendment? Why isn't it the Second Amendment?" Or, "Why should we study about westward movement in the 1800s?" The whole task of the unit should be geared toward answering the essential question. For instance, in the study of geography, an essential question might be, "How does geography affect how and where people live?" In this example, students have to do something with the information—they have to work to integrate what they know with what they can argue is correct. In order for the essential question to work, it has to be highly debatable and answerable insofar as the answer is informed by the thinking and research of the students. In other words, the question itself ends up teaching students to argue, to bring up differing viewpoints, to get engaged, and to ascend the levels of thinking outlined in Bloom's taxonomy. In essence, the teacher is introducing students to a world where there are no right answers: just answers that are informed and supported. Although very often students are much more comfortable in an environment where there are yes and no answers, the proficient social studies teacher will raise questions that allow students to form their own opinions.

Similarly, in terms of selecting and organizing content, it is important to integrate **graphic organizers** into the instruction. If a teacher wants her students to compare and contrast concepts, it is helpful to make a table of whatever the task is and to give that representation to the students. On the other hand, if a teacher has a different goal for the lesson (for instance, synthesis of information), he might choose another type of graphic organizer like a semantic map (or spider web), and this graphic organizer would be geared around another type of question. Social studies teachers also very often demonstrate chronology, analysis, or cause and effect sequence for their students by using graphic organizers. A successful lesson plan often has the material graphically organized for the students so they can learn to think in the way that the graphic organizer is begging.

When it comes to developing **age and grade appropriate learner objectives** in social studies, it is important for the teacher to adjust his or her methods to meet the varying needs of diverse learners. In effect, before beginning a new unit, the teacher must figure out what students know, what they can know, and what the zone of proximal development between the two is. Teachers might administer a pre-assessment before each unit to see where the learners are in an effort to teach to their levels of awareness. This pre-assessment might be a discussion question, an essay response, or a more formal assessment: whatever the means, the proficient social studies teacher will assess the level of awareness that students have in an effort to meet them where they are at. There are also more individualized ways that teachers can check for competence in skills; they can informally assess critical thinking and participation of learners by asking questions and listening to responses. This has long been referred to as the Socratic method, having its origins in the dialogues that the Greek philosopher Socrates had with his students many centuries ago and which are still utilized, particularly in the teaching of law in the universities of the U.S.

Now that we have examined some best practices in social studies as well as overall goals of social studies teachers, we will look at some of the important concepts in social studies when it comes to assessment.

ASSESSMENT IN TEACHING SOCIAL STUDIES

Assessment is the process of gathering information to see if a student or class has made progress in what the teacher has tried to teach. In social studies, assessment can go far beyond formal or traditional methods like **quizzes and tests**. Students can give **oral presentations** on topics or **keep journals** where they reflect on important concepts. They can **write letters to historical figures**, **answer questions**, create **PowerPoint presentations**, **participate in discussions**, and **write papers**. They can **act in skits**, **play games**, and **model events** (like mock trials or negotiations). Finally, they can make **posters and charts** that illustrate the concept the teacher was trying to instruct. All of these methods are effective in actively engaging students in the assessment process. Students can also provide input which can help the teacher design the **rubric** he or she will use to assess.

The key for the social studies teacher is that he or she choose an assessment method that correlates with the purpose of the learning. Very often, the objective addresses the form that the assessment takes. For instance, if you are teaching a lesson about the Scientific Revolution, and your essential question is, "What are the causes and effects of the Scientific Revolution?" then the assessment (an essay, test, or project) is guided by the objective (the essential question initially raised). In short, objectives and assessments are meant to stimulate learning and are intimately intertwined, as if they are two sides to the same coin.

REFERENCES

Adams, D., and Hamm, M. 1998. *Collaborative inquiry in science, math, and technology.* Portsmouth, NH: Heineman.

Discovery Education. 2009. Scientific inquiry 1. Retrieved 2–14–09 at http://school.discoveryeducation.com/lessonplans/programs/scientificInq1/

Geography Education National Implementation Project. 2009. *Geography for life.* Retrieved 2-14-09 from http://genip.tamu.edu/.

Lemlech, J.K. 1994. *Curriculum and instructional methods for the elementary and middle schools.* 3rd ed. New York: Macmillan.

Kasin-Lemlech, J. 1994. *Curriculum and instructional methods for the elementary and middleschool.* 3rd ed. New York: Macmillan.

Kniep, W.M. 1989. "Social Studies Within a Global Education." *Social Education, 53* (Oct. 1989): 399–403.

National Council for the Social Studies. 2009. *Curriculum standards for social studies: II. Thematic strands.* Retrieved December 29, 2008 from www.socialstudies.org/standards/strands.

National Research Council (NRC). 1996. *National science education standards.* Washington, DC: National Academy Press.

National Science Teachers Association. 2002. *NSTA statement: Elementary school science.* Retrieved 2/6/09 from www.nsta.org.

Wood, K.E. 2005. *Interdisciplinary instruction: A practical guide for elementary and middle school teachers.* Upper Saddle River, NJ: Pearson.

Yager, R.E. 2005. *Exemplary science: Best practices in professional development.* Arlington, VA: National Science Teachers' Association Press.

Zemelman, S., Daniels, H., and Hyde, A. (1998). "Best practices for teaching social studies." Best Practice: New standards for teaching and learning in America's schools. Retrieved Jan. 17, 2009 from www.edmond.k12.ok.us/socialstudies

Interdisciplinary Instruction

INTRODUCTION

As opposed to teaching separate subjects, **curriculum integration** encourages team teaching, interdisciplinary instruction, and collaboration among and between teachers and administrators. In this approach, the teacher engages in **interdisciplinary or integrated instruction**, whereby he or she starts with a theme (a topic, problem, question, or main idea) which is then investigated across disciplines.

According to Wood (2005), state lists for learning standards often mention the importance of integrating studies; in fact, some states have even mandated interdisciplinary instruction. So, what exactly does it mean? And how do teachers engage in this methodology?

Wood (2005) tells us that in the early elementary years (especially in kindergarten and grade 1), teachers naturally construct their lessons around themes. For instance, a kindergarten teacher might teach a unit on the seashore by having students copy down letters; investigate animals that live by the sea; draw, circle, and count starfish; etc. The early elementary years seem to lend themselves to this smooth and flowing kind of interdisciplinary inquiry. Nevertheless, as the years progress, teachers often become less inclined to use cross-curricular approaches. However, these approaches are important at all grade levels, which is why they will be explained in depth in this chapter.

THEORY AND APPROACH

The beauty of interdisciplinary instruction is that it becomes an intersecting site for many of the learning theories we've already seen. In essence, the focus of the instruction is that teachers are striving to bring students to perform higher levels of thinking along **Bloom's Taxonomy** (1956). Again, as a point of review, using the taxonomy means assessing learning at different stages of critical thought. For instance, in a Language Arts assignment in which students have to read a story, the teacher might assess at all levels of the taxonomy as follows:

Knowledge: "What's the meaning of the word—?"

Comprehension: "Can someone tell me what the story is about?" Or
   "Please write a summary of the main points in the story."

Application: "Can you use the ideas of the story to explain—?"

Analysis: "Let's try to figure out why—character didn't do—."

Synthesis: "Let's make a plan together to—"

Evaluation: "Which of these three different endings to the story is the best? Why?"

As a general rule, teachers should try to get their students to reach higher levels on the taxonomy.

The interdisciplinary approach is **constructivist** in that teachers are helping students to construct meaning by making connections and finding patterns between and among disciplines. Further, theses units encourage students to socially interact with each other. In the process, students learn valuable skills in terms of cooperation, listening, helping each other, taking on responsibility, negotiating, and making decisions.

What does this approach ask of teachers? In the early elementary grades, it involves individual classroom teachers thinking about what they have to teach across disciplines, making thematic connections, and collaborating with their peers. In the later elementary years, it means interdepartmental interaction and team teaching whereby teachers from different disciplines must plan units in collaboration with other teachers. It may also mean that in the classroom, the teacher will not only need to manage multiple activities of students simultaneously, but also integrate technology into the instruction.

Let's go back to the idea that students will be utilizing the conventional ways of knowing in a specific discipline. What does that mean? Well, if the curricular integration is between science and reading, then the teacher will be using an accepted inquiry approach for the science portion of the unit (such as the scientific method for an experiment and other approaches explained in Chapter 4) and then an accepted approach for reading instruction (such as SQ34 and the other techniques outlined in Chapter 2). When it is integrated well, that kind of overlap is not only seamless, but it also creates meaningful connections in the minds of students.

UNIT AND LESSON PLANNING

The first thing to consider when planning an interdisciplinary unit is the selection of a theme. This theme could emerge from a textbook, a curriculum standard, or even a conversation with another teacher about what he or she is working on in his or her classroom. Some examples for themes might be the environment, transformation, endangered species, and winter. In his chapter "Selecting Fertile Themes for Integrated Learning," D.N. Perkins (cited in Jacobs 1989) argues that effective interdisciplinary themes can be grouped into three categories: change, dependence/independence, and patterns. So perhaps the theme will intersect with one of those broad categories in some way. The theme could be an area of instruction that is part of that year's curriculum or it could be an area that's touched upon year after year but in a much larger way as the student gets older, what Bruner (1963) referred to as "the spiral curriculum." For instance, the theme of the environment may have been examined in a cross-curricular way in earlier grades, but it can be revisited in a more expansive and critical fashion in the upper elementary levels. Prior to settling on the theme, the teacher should consider the developmental and age levels of learners, their prior knowledge of the topic, and the overall learning goals at hand. After finalizing the theme, the unit needs a title, a length, and a set of objectives, lessons, activities, materials, and assessments.

When planning an individual lesson for a unit, the teacher should include short-term and long-term goals (based on district, state, and national standards), instructional objectives, and essential questions (engaging questions of inquiry). In terms of creating lessons, Wood (2005) says that good interdisciplinary lessons have a clear introduction, allow time for students to relate the information to their prior knowledge, engage students in thinking, follow certain methods, include assessments, and have a sense of closure. As an example, perhaps in an interdisciplinary lesson that integrates language arts and social studies, the teachers devise a lesson in which students are asked to imagine that they are back in the time of the Revolutionary War, and they need to write a story discussing their adventures. Creatively, students will have to choose which side they are on (England or the colonists), where they live, what their position is, and how it feels to be in this context. After drafting, students share their lessons with each other in class and work together to revise their pieces, which can ultimately be presented as a means of better understanding the varying contexts for the war.

Jacobs (1989) outlined a step-by-step approach for designing interdisciplinary curriculum. The first step, "selecting an organizing center," involves picking a topic, which can be a theme, subject area, event, issue, or problem. The second step, "brainstorming associations," means mapping out the unit of study by putting the topic in the middle and branching off with the different disciplines and how they will be investigating the topic. Jacobs (1989) further explains that in step three, questions need to be established which will guide the unit by serving as its scope and sequence. When the questions are developed, the final step is "writing activities for implementation," which asks the teachers to examine the questions and identify tasks they will require from the students. These tasks should correlate with the stages of Bloom's Taxonomy. Jacobs explains that teachers should employ a variety of methods when making up these activities—methods which take into account the diversity of learning modalities. Moreover, the activities should reflect a balance between a wide variety of methods, including lecture, group projects, discussion, and research.

As was previously stated, Jacobs (1989) asserts how important it is for teachers who are working together to meet and brainstorm about their ideas, ideally on a concept map. Wood (2005) articulates the same notion. The **concept maps** or webs that they talk about are graphic organizers that allow viewers to understand how the theme is going to be implemented across disciplines and what distinct approaches will be used. The following is a sample interdisciplinary unit plan which is intended for early elementary learners and uses the concept map approach:

Figure 5.1 Fall: An Interdisciplinary Approach

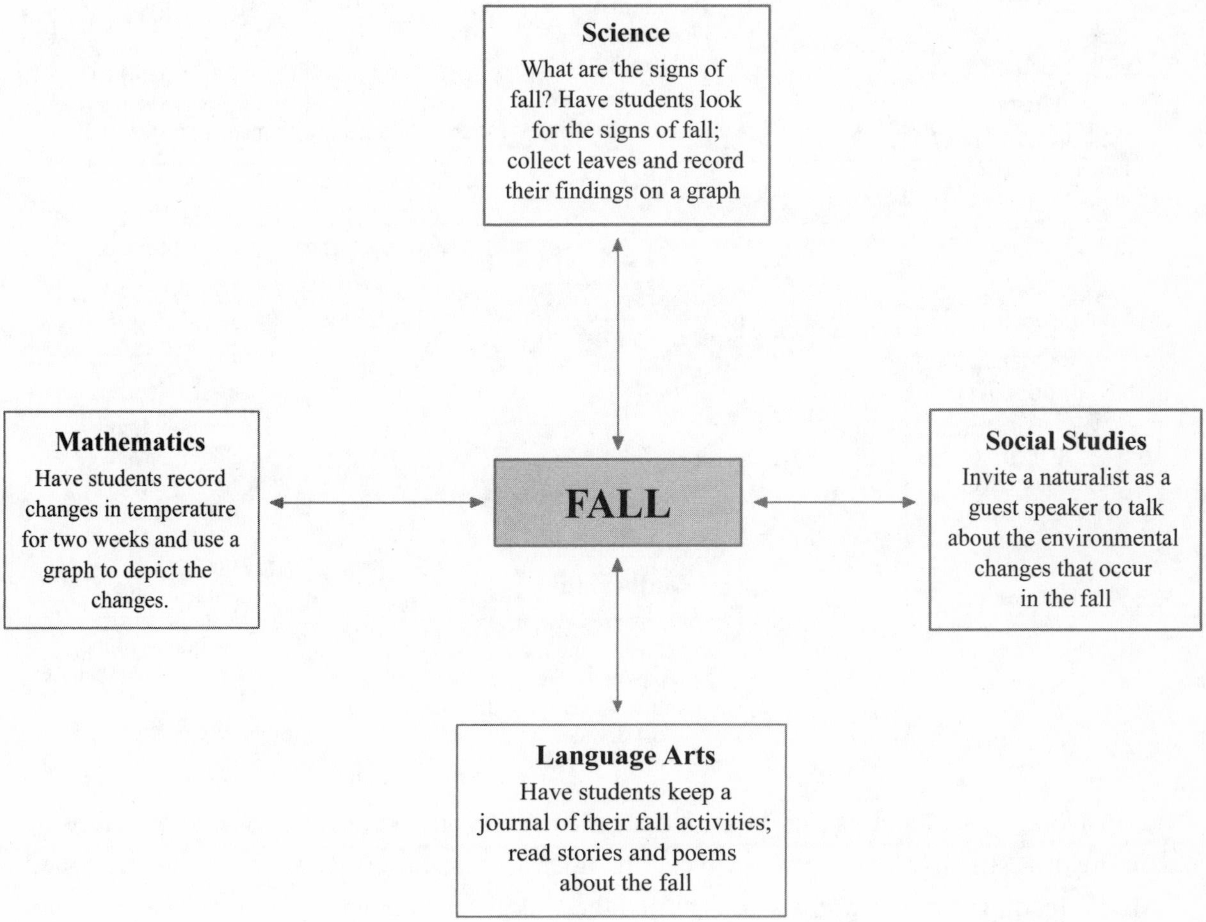

Science
What are the signs of fall? Have students look for the signs of fall; collect leaves and record their findings on a graph

Mathematics
Have students record changes in temperature for two weeks and use a graph to depict the changes.

FALL

Social Studies
Invite a naturalist as a guest speaker to talk about the environmental changes that occur in the fall

Language Arts
Have students keep a journal of their fall activities; read stories and poems about the fall

Since the planning process is so integral to integrated instruction, another example of concept mapped planning is included for your review. In this case, the example concerns a third grade unit on the rainforest.

Figure 5.2 The Brazilian Rainforest

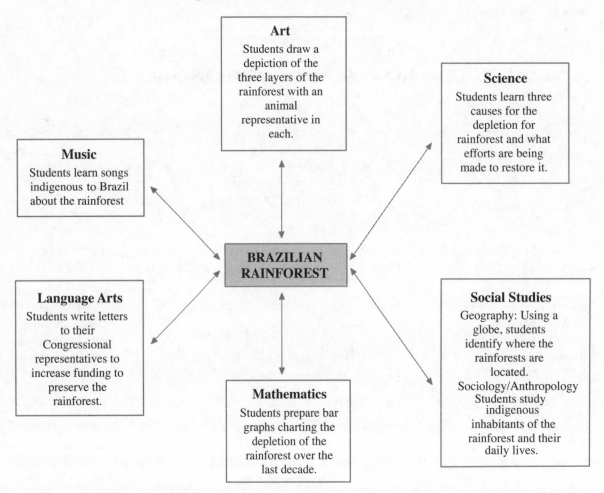

Wood (2005) asserts that in the upper elementary grades, the units will probably be more investigative or research-driven. In other words, now that students have learned basic reading, writing, and research skills, these skills can be put to the test. The approach to planning the unit is the same: the teachers select the theme for the unit, align that theme with the learning standards, evaluate resources, meet as a team to brainstorm a concept map, develop essential questions, and then determine what activities can be developed with respect to the questions along different levels of Bloom's Taxonomy.

For instance, perhaps in a fifth grade class, students are studying westward expansion, and a group of teachers collaboratively decide on that topic for the theme of the interdisciplinary unit. These teachers might decide on a specific essential question to guide the learning, such as "What forces led pioneers to seek out a life in the West?" Jacobs (1997) asserts that the essential question should be debatable and thought-provoking. Similarly, Wiggins and McTighe (1998) mention that through examining the essential question, students arrive at a deeper understanding of a concept: in this case it might be that there are a variety of political, cultural, religious, and social forces that intersect and propel people to migrate. Then, the teachers proceed to think about how different disciplines might investigate that theme. The teachers meet and develop a concept map which might include activities such as making maps of Lewis and Clark's journey (Social Studies); examining plants, animals, and ecosystems encountered during expansion (Science); reading books about Native Americans and writing reports about famous pioneers (Language Arts); and looking at supply and demand as it relates to the gold rush (Economics/Mathematics). The teachers align those activities with different levels of the taxonomy. For instance, students might recall the geographic locations that Lewis and Clark traveled to, and then towards the higher end, students could analyze the influence that Native Americans had on their voyage, such as learning about hunting and cooking. Students might also identify a decision Lewis and Clark made along their journey and evaluate that decision.

Among the variety of alternative approaches to integrated curriculum design set forth by Fogarty (2002), one that is worth mentioning is the **threaded approach**. In this method, the team of teachers selects a particular critical-thinking skill (such as "compare and contrast"), cooperative skill ("taking turns"), study skill, organizing skill, multiple intelligence, or standard that is threaded through a variety of disciplines. For instance, in a unit on "compare and contrast," students in language arts might compare and contrast two stories, while in social studies they might compare the causes of World War I with the causes of World War II. Again, teachers work in cross-disciplinary teams, but in this case they devise units around the selected skill, standard, or multiple intelligence level.

ASSESSMENT IN INTERDISCIPLINARY INSTRUCTION

In interdisciplinary instruction, a variety of assessment methods should be used, but generally speaking, the teachers should use a project-based learning pedagogy—in other words, one that is collaborative and active with clear roles and problem-solving of a tangible outcome. Very often, **oral exposition**, which emphasizes the interaction of interdisciplinary information, is important to measure.

Teachers should consider other methods as well. **Portfolios** can include examples of student work, journal entries, and self-evaluations. **Graphic organizers**, **oral presentations**, **posters**, **interviews**, **performances**, **exhibitions**, and more traditional measurements like **tests** and **quizzes** can be used.

Undoubtedly, assessments can cross disciplines. For instance, imagine that a social studies instructor and a language arts instructor have collaborated on a unit about abolitionism. As a means of assessment, both teachers could ask the students to write speeches. Perhaps half of the class would express their views as if they were abolitionists, and the other half of the class could write from the perspective of people who want to preserve slavery as an institution. In this example, students must utilize knowledge of the abolitionist movement as well as language arts skills like making a speech, recognizing the concerns of an audience, and writing and revising. The assessment might also lead further inquiry into the matter and perhaps even a debate.

In their book *Understanding by Design,* Wiggins and McTighe (1998) outline the backwards design approach—individuals who design curriculum begin by figuring out what they want students to know and then working backwards to the learning experiences and instruction needed to get there. These researchers assert that performance tasks and projects which are "open-ended, complex, and authentic" forms of assessment lead to more enduring understanding than traditional tests and quizzes do. Undoubtedly, a variety of assessment techniques should be integrated into the interdisciplinary plan in an effort to put forth a balanced approach to the learning, but special emphasis should be given to the performance tasks and projects that Wiggins and McTighe (1998) discuss.

PRAXIS Pointer

Relax. Bring your shoulders up to your ears, hold for 10 seconds—release and relax. Do this 2–3 times. Then try it with other muscles in your body.

As Jacobs (1989) asserts, interdisciplinary instruction is very important for educators to utilize because it fosters deeper understanding of the subject, improved problem-solving, and greater transfer of knowledge from one discipline to another. Jacobs (1989) also stresses that these approaches make students more hands-on and self-directed in their learning; moreover, they will see the connections between what they are studying and what is going on in the world around them.

REFERENCES

Bruner, J. 1963. *Acts of meaning*. Cambridge, MA: Harvard UP.

Fogarty, R. 2002. How to integrate the curricula. 2nd ed. Arlington Heights, Ill: Skylight Professional Development.

Jacobs, H.H. 1989. *Interdisciplinary curriculum: Design and implementation.* Alexandria, VA: The Association for Supervision and Curriculum Development.

————. *Mapping the big picture: Integrating curriculum & assessment K-12.* Alexandria,VA: The Association for Supervision and Curriculum Development.

Wiggins, G. and McTighe, J. 1998. *Understanding by design*. Alexandria, VA: The Association for Supervision and Curriculum Development.

Wood, K.E. 2005. *Interdisciplinary instruction: A practical guide for elementary and middle school teachers*. Upper Saddle River, NJ: Pearson.

Practice Tests 1 & 2

INTRODUCTION

This chapter contains two practice tests, each of which has four constructed response questions. To answer the questions completely, give yourself thirty minutes for each question for a total of two hours. Before you begin the practice tests, you may want to review the section in Chapter 1 on the format of the test beginning on page 5. In addition, we have provided below the *ETS Scoring Guide* (Elementary Education Content Area Exercises 0012 Test-at-a-Glance page 2) which the scorers use when reading the exams. You can see how each iteration of the scoring rubric changes according to the completeness and demonstration of your knowledge.

Scoring Guide

Score of 6: Answers *all* parts of the exercise clearly and successfully. Demonstrates a superior understanding of the subject matter, human growth and development, and pedagogy required by the exercise. Provides coherent, well-organized, and fully developed explanations of key ideas. And, gives clean, well-chosen examples or supporting details.

Score of 5: Answers *all important* parts of the exercise clearly and successfully. Demonstrates a strong understanding of the subject matter, human growth and development and pedagogy required by the exercise. Provides coherent organized and developed explanations of key ideas. Gives clear and relevant examples or supporting details.

Score of 4: Answers *all* important parts of the exercise adequately. Demonstrates an accurate if somewhat limited understanding of the subject matter human growth and development and pedagogy required by the exercise. Provides clear appropriate explanations of key ideas. Gives relevant examples or supporting details.

Score of 3: Answers *only some* parts of the exercise adequately. Demonstrates some understanding of the subject matter human growth and development and pedagogy required by the exercise with few serious inaccuracies. Provides explanations of key ideas but they lack clarity and depth. Gives only some relevant examples or supporting details.

Score of 2: Answers *no* parts of the exercise adequately and only some in a limited way. Demonstrates a limited understanding of the content required by the exercise. May provide explanations but they are unclear and/ or undeveloped. May give examples or details but they contain inaccuracies.

Score of 1: Answers *no* part of the exercise adequately. Demonstrates a serious lack of knowledge in the areas required by the exercise. May have such serious problems in organization and development that the response is generally incoherent. May give no accurate examples or supporting details.

Score of 0: Answer is blank, off-topic, or illegible.

Remember to replicate the actual exam environment and be sure to time yourself so that you get used to organizing your thoughts and answering the questions thoroughly. After you complete the each practice test you will find sample responses representing a six-point and two-point score.

PRACTICE TEST 1: CONSTRUCTED RESPONSE QUESTIONS

Question 1—Language Arts

TIME: 30 minutes

Scenario: *In a class of 20 4th grade students, five are reading two grade levels above, ten are reading at grade level, and five are reading 1–2 grade levels below. How would you create a meaningful comprehension lesson that reaches all students? The lesson must illustrate the principles of a balanced reading program. Explain how you will ensure that reading comprehension is addressed. Specifically, describe a pre-reading activity you would use with a text, two instructional techniques that you would use to bolster comprehension of a story, and a post-reading activity that would help assess comprehension.*

Question 2—Mathematics

TIME: 30 minutes

Scenario: *In a third grade math class of 20 students, seven struggle with word problems, but within that subset three also lack basic computation skills. Describe activities that would help these students with their specific difficulties. Provide examples of what the students would do and how you would assess them given these two unique classroom challenges.*

Question 3—Science

TIME: 30 minutes

Scenario: *In a fifth grade science class, students were brought to a local pond and asked to record their observations. Unfortunately for the teacher, the students were disinterested and unruly at the pond. Given this description, how would you redesign this activity in order to engage learners in the scientific method?*

Question
4—Interdisciplinary Instruction

TIME: 30 minutes

Scenario: *In a sixth grade interdisciplinary unit on the theme "civilization," the social studies teacher is discussing Ancient Mesopotamia; the language arts teacher is overseeing the research paper; the math teacher is conducting lessons on understanding the basic economic principles of the Sumerians; and the science teacher is focusing on their basic technological advancements. Overall, these teachers are trying to get students to understand the scope of the Sumerian civilization in terms of economic, social, religious, and political influences.*

Explain how you would incorporate learning activities with an emphasis on the goals of social studies and language arts; specifically, how would you use writing and engage learners in collaborative learning techniques?

PRACTICE TEST 1:
CONSTRUCTED RESPONSE SAMPLE ANSWERS

Question 1: Language Arts
Six-Point Response

Generally speaking, I would devise a balanced approach to teaching reading. Specifically, I would frequently assess my students as to their level so they could be placed into appropriate reading groups and they could move into and out of groups as needed. In this approach I would combine my use of whole-class guided texts with having students put into guided reading groups where the texts are on different levels according to ability. Ideally, the guided reading group texts would be united according to theme but differentiated according to the pre-assessed levels of students. For targeted strategies in comprehension, there are times when the teacher might use homogeneous grouping. In my classroom, there will be many times when I will use heterogeneous grouping, but given this particular situation, I would utilize homogeneous grouping in an effort to let students work on similar goals and to share strengths.

In terms of pre-reading, I would establish a purpose for reading through KWL, vocabulary introduction, and/or discussion of ideas that will acquaint readers with the background knowledge required for their text. I would conduct these pre-reading activities with the entire class. Then, I would homogeneously divide this group of 20 into smaller groups (five each) based on reading ability. I would initiate a guided reading program by using appropriately leveled reading materials for each of the groups. Likewise, I would set individualized goals for each of the groups.

When it comes to the lower-level reading group, I would focus their efforts on working on decoding and predicting strategies. I would take advantage of the opportunities for reciprocal reading among these learners in an effort to get them questioning, summarizing, clarifying, and predicting. I would have these students do some extensive vocabulary preparation activities so they are ready before they read. They would also have the text read aloud to them before they read it silently. I would outline some of the big ideas, supporting details, and content for them in a graphic organizer, parts of which would be left blank for the students to complete. I would also work on some decoding practice for the tougher words in the text. I would provide consistent and frequent assessment by observing them as they read the text softly or silently to themselves and as they read the text orally. Finally, I would check in with them for understanding and comprehension.

For the middle groups (in this scenario, there are two groups with five students in each group), I would focus on the goal of them making connections between their texts and other texts we've read. While I would use many of the aforementioned strategies, I would encourage partner reading activities as well as more independent reading. I would create graphic organizers for them which would allow them to make those intertextual connections.

I would encourage the group of five who are reading two grade levels above to work on higher level skills along Bloom's Taxonomy such as making inferences and evaluations about their assigned text. These students would be encouraged to do more pair-share reading and more independent work. I would devise a graphic organizer with higher level questions asking them to synthesize what they have read. Perhaps I would engage them by asking them to illustrate the theme of the book in a different form. For instance, perhaps they would compose a short story or a poem that allows them to articulate their understanding of the theme.

While providing this kind of guidance to a specific group, I would ensure that other students in the other groups are engaged in active learning of their specific literacy activity. In terms of post-reading activities, I would observe and provide guidance to individual students and differentiate my instruction by asking different kinds of questions of each student based on individual need. I would also ask specific questions to ensure that each text has been comprehended by the students. Given this homogeneous grouping, the assessment would take place through my observation of group work and through quizzes, tests, and student projects. Of course, these assessments would be individualized to the learning goals of the specific groups.

Two-Point Response

If I were assigned this particularly diverse group of learners, I would select a whole-class text that illustrated the theme of the unit I was working on. This text would be leveled with the middle group of readers, thus challenging the lower level and serving as reinforcement of skills for the higher level readers. I would present lessons that informed students of the background and context of the text. One of my activities would be to put students into groups and have them discuss their impressions of the story. This open-ended method would encourage creativity and engagement on the part of the students. In order to assess this activity and their comprehension, I would make anecdotal notes about their input. I would also include vocabulary building lessons to help all of the students increase their reading skills. Finally, I would integrate round-robin reading into our class. I would select an interesting or difficult part of the text and then ask each student to read a few sentences of it as we went around the room.

After reading the book, we'd do a full class discussion of the book based on questions I came up with. For post-reading, I would ask students to respond to an essay question based on a major theme of the book that I would have helped them to identify. I'd also have them take a multiple-choice test on the book to assess comprehension. If students encountered difficulty in answering the questions, they would be directed to reread the text. Through these activities, I am confident that all of the students would have better comprehension of the text.

(This answer has limitations. The writer lists literacy activities without explaining how or why she would choose and/or use them. Some of the activities do not actually help with or assess comprehension.)

Question 2: Mathematics
Six-Point Response

Generally, third grade math students need rapid recall of facts coupled with a conceptual understanding of what those facts mean. If I were the teacher in this scenario, I would tackle each problem separately by devising specific approaches for each of the unique challenges presented. The following essay will elaborate on what those approaches would be.

Regarding the seven students who struggle with word problems, I would connect with the reading specialist in the school to discuss the situation. I would show him or her the word problems that the students didn't get and ask him or her to help me come up with specific strategies to address their needs. After seeking this professional assessment of the problem, I would couple the recommendations with some of my own techniques to foster decoding skills among the learners. I would teach them how to isolate and circle key words in the word problem (words like "calculate" or "compare numbers"). I would have the students define these words and then make a chart of them—one that they could refer to during the test. I would also model for them how they could break the question down by representing it graphically. After showing them how they could draw pictures and graphs of the problem, I would assign problems to them and ask them to draw out what the question is asking.

In terms of the students who lack computation skills, I would strike a balance between direct instruction and individual practice. With computation, I would isolate weak skill areas, do real life as well as theoretical examples with students, and use manipulatives. For instance, if the computation problem concerns addition or subtraction facts in third grade, I would let the students deepen their understanding of the concept by using base-ten blocks that allow them to count. Then, I would encourage more practice with basic recall of facts (such as "fact tests" in which students have to solve a sheet of problems under the time constraint of a minute, or computational games for the class to play). Finally, I would encourage my students to check their work for computation errors, and I would allow class time for that kind of activity.

Two-Point Response

It is very important for students to understand the four main arithmetic operations. Addition means "unite two numbers in a sum." Subtraction means remove or take away a number, where the result is called a difference. Multiplication and division are the other two operations, and they are inverses of each other, although in multiplication the result is a product, while in division the result is a quotient.

As the teacher of basic computational skills, I would encourage calculator games which would allow students to use calculators to compute. Using the calculator is an important and lifelong skill which transcends math into other disciplines like science. It is also a meaningful way to support computational weakness. In essence, computations can be challenging for students, and it is very important to show them how they can use technological advances like the calculator to find the solution to basic math problems.

Regarding the students who are struggling with word problems, I would have them practice with more problems or read the problems aloud. I think that having students read the problems aloud would help them understand the underlying concepts at hand.

(This response is unclear, undeveloped, and limited in terms of answering the question. It shows an incomplete understanding of content and pedagogy and has major errors—calculators aren't supposed to be used to teach computation; rather, they are intended to support higher order thinking in mathematics. Similarly, reading word problems out loud will not help students to understand them.)

Question 3: Science
Six-Point Response

First, I would get the students invested in and excited about the exercise. I would show a list with pictures of some of the organisms that were found in previous years. Together, the students could discuss and come up with a testable hypothesis that they all want to discuss. For instance, the hypothesis could be that in warmer portions of the pond there are more living creatures that may be found. (Note: this may or may not be proven correct).

The next step would be to keep the students excited in the field. Prior to leaving for the pond, I would have the students prepare a data sheet for taking samples. For example, I would teach them that when they take the sample they will have to record the temperature, the date, time, weather conditions, depth of sample, etc. Therefore, they will have an easy guide to help in their observations. When the students sample the pond water, they can either use a field lens or the naked eye to identify organisms in the water. Any organisms found may be catalogued on their data sheet and placed in a sample bag or jar.

Finally, the students will bring the water samples and any organisms found back to the lab. Using microscopes, they will discover that some samples which appeared to be devoid of organisms are teeming with them. I would then tally on the whiteboard the number and type of organism by temperature. Then, I would ask them to evaluate whether their hypothesis was true or false. Lastly, I would encourage the students to ask why that is the case and to draw conclusions. This step can be completed even if their hypothesis ended up being false. In the end, I will encourage them to come up with a conclusion that fits with the data they observed.

Two-Point Response

The first thing I would do is ask the students what they expect to observe at the pond. I would have them discuss this and then I would write their expectations on the whiteboard. I would then distribute field books to the students prior to leaving for the trip. I would instruct the students to observe everything they see at the pond and to write that down in their field books. I would instruct them to make sure they use the scientific method in their observations.

Once they return to the classroom, I would have the students discuss what they did see. I would then write the results of what they saw on the whiteboard. I would then compare what we expected to see with what we did see. I would have the students then conclude why there was a difference between what we expected to observe and what we actually observed.

(This response demonstrates a very limited understanding in the scientific method. Although the responder does try to get the students to articulate what they think they will see beforehand, there is no hypothesis produced which can be objectively tested. Instead, the responder is just comparing what the students expected to see with what they did see.)

Question 4: Interdisciplinary Instruction
Six-Point Response

As a teacher in this class, I would first gauge the students in terms of their interest areas and strengths. Then I would put them in small groups based on the cultural topics which interconnect with their interests. In these groups, the students would engage in inquiry-based approaches; they would generate questions and hypotheses about their specific areas of Mesopotamian civilization. Each group would generate a list of subtopics, and each student would take ownership of one. For instance, students in the economics group might branch off into the areas of economic classes, products, money and banking, etc., as they pertain to Mesopotamia. Students would go to the library and conduct Internet research from a list of pre-determined websites. I would also provide mini-lessons on different strategies for note-taking and source evaluation. Then, the students would each write a component to what would become (when combined) a short research paper on their topic. Students would present their papers in class.

As a secondary activity, I would use the jigsaw technique whereby they would come together in heterogeneous groups. In these groups, each student would now be an expert in her or his area, and they would have the responsibility to collaboratively teach their other group members what they have learned about their topic (such as "Economics of Mesopotamia"). The goal of this jigsaw activity would be for students to contribute their areas of expertise to a student-created website or wiki. Again, this project would involve note-taking, writing, and collaboration among team members.

These two activities would allow students to see how the information they have learned intersects with the research conducted by other students, which in turn would gives them a much fuller understanding of the larger theme: civilization.

Two-Point Response

I would suggest that the social studies teacher should conduct a series of lectures on all aspects of Sumerian culture. For instance, the teacher might mention how Mesopotamia is the most ancient civilization known to man. Furthermore, he or she should mention how it is significant that, like so many other major societies, the Sumerians settled around bodies of water. In this case, Mesopotamia was founded between two rivers, the Tigris and the Euphrates. The Sumerians were one of the first people to live on this fertile land. The social studies teacher should also instruct the students about the time frame when this civilization came to pass (from 3500–2000 B.C.) and how the Sumerians were the founders of modern civilization in that they developed an alphabet (cuneiform), they had an army with weapons, they studied math and science, they made vehicles with wheels, and they had a society with three classes (wealthy, working class, and slaves). After the students take notes on the lecture, the social studies teacher should test them on their knowledge.

In terms of the contributions of the language arts teacher, he or she should create a central research question for the students to understand, such as "How did Mesopotamia reflect all aspects of culture?" Then, he or she should encourage all of the students to write an answer to that question. In terms of teaching the research process, the language arts teacher should encourage all of the students to learn the same note-taking system: using note cards. The teacher should bring the students to the library for an individual consultation and a guided tour of the best sources to use.

Collaboratively, both teachers should gather and have the students watch the same informative video on Sumerian culture. Then, they should cooperate with each other to create a pencil and paper exam to be given at the end of the unit.

(This answer is insufficient because it encourages strictly lecture-based as opposed to inquiry-based instruction for social studies; it encourages only traditional assessment methods; it allows for only one approach to the note-taking process; and in general, it is teacher-centered as opposed to student-centered in terms of instruction. It provides an incomplete understanding of pedagogy as it relates to the area of integrated instruction.)

PRACTICE TEST 2: CONSTRUCTED RESPONSE QUESTIONS

Question 1—Language Arts

TIME: 30 minutes

Scenario: *In a fourth grade classroom, students are writing short (one to two paragraphs) narrative pieces. Here is a sample of one student's work:*

SAMPLE:

I began walking to the large airport from the big airplane.
We had to go on a tram. I held tight to my mothers hand.
I was so excited to see my grandparents.

How would you support this student through the writing process? What direct instruction is needed? What kind of support? What writing goals do you have as her classroom teacher? How will you measure if they are achieved?

Question 2—Mathematics

TIME: 30 minutes

Scenario: *You are teaching a third grade class multiplication of two- and three-digit numbers. You find out that half the class does not even remember the concept of place value. The students who understand these concepts would be bored if you were to re-teach these concepts.*

(a) *Give* two *activities that will explain the concept of place value for the students that do not remember it and be sure to explain the activities in terms of what is known about how children learn mathematics.*

(b) *Give* two *activities that can prepare the half of the class for the multiplication of two- and three-digit numbers and be sure to justify your choices in terms of what is known about how children learn mathematics.*

Question 3—Social Studies

TIME: 30 minutes

Scenario: *You are about to begin teaching a unit on World War II to your sixth grade students. Describe four writing activities other than a research paper that you could assign to students to get them interested in and excited about the lesson. Explain the reasons for your choices.*

Question 4—Interdisciplinary Instruction

TIME: 30 minutes

Scenario: *A science and social studies teacher decide that they want to work together on an interdisciplinary unit for their sixth grade students. As a teacher, structure a project that intersects science and social studies and focuses on a relevant, real world issue. Be sure to include instructional and assessment strategies. Mention how you will support students with learning differences.*

Question 1: Language Arts
Six-Point Response

As the teacher, I would develop a structured writing experience to help students revise their work. In my class, a paragraph like this one would have been generated from prompts that encouraged students to write about different subjects. I would include mini-lessons on process, content, and grammar/editing. In terms of teaching the writing process, I would encourage all of the students to build sensory details around specific moments. I would encourage them to add details through brainstorming. I would also encourage them to develop multiple drafts.

In terms of direct instruction, I would review topic sentence formation with the class. I would share how I solve similar problems with formulating my own topic sentences in my own writing. If I have the opportunity, I might expand this lesson to include a visit from a "real author" who could describe solving such dilemmas. I would also go over the use of narrative transition words such as "next" and "then." With respect to the grammar and editing that needs to take place, I would look at sentence structure with the students and teach skills as they arise in the paragraphs. I would also integrate technology into my teaching; in this case, I would have students use programs to help them brainstorm ideas, organize details, and practice grammar skills.

My classes would include oral conferences with students and structured peer review. I would encourage my students to read their writing aloud to me, to analyze models of sample paragraphs, to revise and edit, and then eventually to participate in with the class by using the author's chair technique whereby at the end of this experience students take turns presenting their work and getting feedback.

In terms of assessment, I would compare the final draft to prior drafts, use a rubric that focuses on the areas I am targeting, and also have students engage in self-evaluation. I would try to build in a way to celebrate the final draft through publishing it for a wider audience. Ultimately the piece would become part of the portfolio which is used to evaluate the student's writing over time.

Two-Point Response

This assignment would be generated from a writing prompt I would have assigned to the entire class: tell me about a special moment in your life.

I would provide direct instruction to the student by encouraging her to add details to this paragraph. I would have all of the students trade papers and mark up editing. I would bring the students through one more draft in the writing process. In terms of assessment, I would grade this paragraph in terms of how it stands in comparison to the other paragraphs that students handed in, with a particular emphasis on how well the students have edited and adhered to the rules of grammar.

(There are many reasons why this answer is insufficient. Aside from being incomplete, the writing prompt is solely teacher-generated, there is no use of a rubric, no conferencing, no portfolio review, and no integration of technology.)

Question 2: Mathematics
Six-Point Response

In order for the students to understand the abstract concept of place values in concrete terms, I would use base-10 blocks. I would have the students explain to me what a cube represents (the 1s place) and what the rod represents (the 10s place). In this way the students are able to understand the concept of place value. Once I assessed that the students were comfortable with the base-10 blocks, I could move on to a number game.

In this instance, I would have students make three cards: one each with a 1, a 10, and a 100 on it. I would write a three-digit number on the board (say, 532). I would ask the students to raise the place value card with the three in it. I could then assess which students raised the 10 card and which did not and needed further help.

A great game would be a fact review of single-digit multiplication. I would break the students into pairs, with a deck of cards for every pair. Each student would throw a card down (suit cards equal 10) and the first one to shout the fact would win. If there is a three and an eight, the first one to say twenty-four wins. Students enjoy learning with games that are within the appropriate ability. This not only reviews multiplication facts but also challenges them to remember with speed.

A second activity to prepare the students for two- and three-digit multiplication would be to have the students make up word problems which could be solved by the class later. I would model this activity by creating a question for students to solve: *In our class of 20 students, each student has a deck of cards with 52 cards in each. How many cards does the class have?* After they set up the equation and solved the problem, I would put them in pairs and ask each duo to come up with a word problem. This type of activity allows students to relate mathematics to everyday life and enables them to understand how to convert word problems to math problems and back again. Moreover, they would definitely enjoy creating their problems and having them solved by the class.

Two-Point Response

I could have the students who did not know how to use place values make cards with place values on them so they would see concretely what the place values are. Another activity would be to pair the students who did not have trouble with place values with the students who did not understand. This is because students learn well from their peers.

To keep the other students busy while I am reviewing the place value material, I could give several worksheets to the students who know place value. This would keep them busy and help them learn through repetition. Overall, the students who know place values could teach it to the students who do not remember what place values are.

(This answer received a two because it is too concise, very weak on details and does not show very much understanding about how children learn. Although the writer mentions using cards as concrete examples, the writer does not explain how the cards will be used.)

Question 3: Social Studies
Six-Point Response

If I were teaching a unit on World War II, I would engage in a variety of approaches to help students become aware of the war and its legacy. For instance, I'd want students to know about the major aspects of the war (the Treaty of Versailles, the Great Depression, the rise of totalitarianism, the formation of alliances, the invasive advances of Germany/Italy/Japan, the two fronts in Europe and the Pacific, and the Holocaust). I would want the students to gain a deeper understanding of how political boundaries change over time and place.

One writing activity that I would assign would be for them to write a paper describing what the state of the world would be today if Germany and the Axis powers had defeated the United States and the Allies in World War II. This is an exciting exercise for the students as it requires a great deal of imagination. It also gives them a great lesson on how the past helps to shape the current world. It also requires a great deal of knowledge about history as they would have to make sure they understood the political structure at the end of the war.

Another excellent writing activity that I would recommend would be to research what life as like for different individuals impacted by the war. In essence, I would have them write from the point of view of an American soldier, a Jewish person in Poland, or a Japanese-American in an internment camp. I would explain to the students how we often talk about events and famous people in the past but we also need to examine what life was like for an average person. I would have them describe what their job was, what foods they ate, etc. This activity allows them to utilize their creativity which will make the historical time period come alive for them.

A third writing activity I would use would be to have students write two news accounts of Pearl Harbor. One account would be told from the perspective of the Americans, and the other would be told from the perspective of the Japanese. As an activity, we could write these accounts as scripts that would be broadcast over the radio, and we could act it out. They will also begin to understand that one view of history may not be the same as the point of view of someone from another country.

Finally, I would ask students to interview someone who lived during World War II. I would have the students get an account of where the person was during that time period and what he or she remembers. To frame this activity, I would invite a guest speaker who was a veteran of World War II to come to speak to the class.

Two-Point Response

World War II was a devastating event in history that changed the world. If I were teaching a unit on World War II, I would have the students write a newspaper article about one aspect of it so they could understand about World War II. I would also have the students write a short skit about World War II.

(This author received a 2 because although these may be good activities for the students, there is little or no explanation about the reason for the choices. It is difficult to see the connections to themes that the teacher is trying to make.)

Question 4: Interdisciplinary Instruction
Six-Point Response

I think that it would be meaningful for these educators to create a collaborate project around the theme "Energy Conservation." This unit would utilize project-based learning pedagogy—it would be collaborative and active, students would be assigned clear roles for solving problems, and there would be an oral exposition component which emphasizes the interdisciplinary connections the teachers are trying to make. In this case, the project would culminate in a community exposition where students would present their ideas orally to parents and other invited guests.

I would begin with this essential question: "What societal and environmental forces have led to the need for energy conservation?" In my cross-curricular discussions, I would stress that the deeper understanding I want them to have is how economic, political, and environmental influences have converged in ways that makes the need for energy conservation urgent and paramount.

In this project, students would work in heterogeneous groups. I would encourage that outcomes be teacher-guided and differentiated by both ability and interest. Inevitably, the social studies and science teachers would work together to plan collaborative lessons which they would team teach. The social studies teacher would provide direct instruction about the sociological and historical issues surrounding energy conservation; but he or she could also integrate nonfiction and fiction readings and lead discussions on such topics as why oil prices have risen, the effects of rising energy costs, the history of energy usage, etc. I think that the science teacher would use the same kind of inquiry-based approach, focusing his or her science lessons on issues such as "What is energy?", "What are the various forms of energy?", and "What are the various methods of conserving energy?"

As a group, the students participating in this learning experience would take on different roles for their public exhibitions, but all of them would be required to research an area of interest that ties together understandings in both science and social studies. I would ask them to create joint PowerPoint presentations which would illustrate their research. I would require that the presentations have graphs that show scientific data, well-written explanations, and historic timelines of events that connect to each other. These presentations would be assessed by using a rubric that the teachers collaborate upon. After the presentations are completed, as a larger group we would create a model of an energy-efficient structure—a house, business, or car—that the students would select and research. Eventually, students would be asked to orally defend this structure in a follow-up public forum.

Two-Point Response

In this case, the social studies teacher would work with the theme of how the environment is affected by people as they interact with it, while the science teacher would focus his efforts on discussing what energy is. The teachers would work on projects in each of their classes. Each teacher would devise his or her methods to assess the learning as it pertains to his or her domain.

(The limitations here are multifold: teachers work in isolation, no big ideas to unite information, no essential questions are raised, no joint projects are put forth, isolated activities are suggested, etc.)

Index